WHEN DOES WAR BECOME CRIME?
ASPECTS OF THE CRIMINAL CASE AGAINST ERIC O.

A Challenge for European Law:
The Merging of Internal and External Security

When does War become Crime?
Aspects of the Criminal Case against Eric O.

Diede-Jan Dieben and Thom Dieben

With a Foreword by Professor Elspeth Guild

CMR

When does War become Crime? Aspects of the Criminal Case against Eric O.
Diede-Jan Dieben and Thom Dieben
ISBN: 90-5850-139-6

Wolf Legal Publishers (WLP)
P.O. Box 31051
6503 CB Nijmegen
The Netherlands

Orders for this book can be mailed to wlp@hetnet.nl
More information and prices at www.wlp.biz

Layout: Hannie van de Put

Foreword

This book forms part of CHALLENGE (The Changing Landscape of European Liberty and Security) a research project funded by the European Commission under its Sixth Framework Research Programme (Theme 6.1.1 of Priority 7, "Citizens and Governance in a Knowledge based society"). CHALLENGE is a tool for setting high standards of intellectual debate around security and liberty in Europe. CHALLENGE brings together 23 universities and institutes in the Member States, representing a valuable instrument for policy recommendations, which contributes to the development of an EU Area of Freedom Security and Justice. It runs for a period of five years starting from 1st June 2004.

CHALLENGE seeks to facilitate a more responsive and responsible assessment of rules and practices of security. It examines the implications of these practices for civil liberties, human rights and social cohesion in an enlarged Europe. The project analyses the illiberal practices of liberal regimes and challenges their justification on grounds of emergency and necessity. Among the objectives of the project the following may be highlighted: To understand the merging between internal and external security and evaluate the changing character of the relationship between liberty and security in Europe; To analyse the role of different institutions in charge of security and their current transformations; To facilitate and enhance a new interdisciplinary network of scholars who have been influential in the re-conceptualising and analysis of many of the theoretical, political, sociological, legal and policy implications of new forms of violence and political identity; and to bring together a new interdisciplinary network of scholars in an integrated project focusing on the state of exception as enacted through illiberal practices and forms of resistance to it.

The Radboud University of Nijmegen, as one of the partners in CHALLENGE, has launched a series of research studies into the relationship in law of actions taken by the military abroad and criminal law in the Member States. In order better to understand the meaning of internal and external security for Europe, the institutions which are engaged in security and their actions need to be analysed. The institutions which are primarily responsible for security are the police within the state and the army as regards the external world. While the worlds in which they engage are separated by the border of sovereignty, their objective of providing security is defined foremost by their duty to protect the people and the state to which they belong and by which they are paid. Thus the police owe a duty of protection to the people they police and the military owe a duty of protection to their citizens and state. The mechanisms, practices and technologies available to each of these two institutions are different (though there is increasing overlap). They are subject to different legal regimes as regards the legality of their actions – the police are answerable for their actions within the criminal justice systems of the Member States, the military are judged by their own separate courts.

'Europe', however, is changing our understanding of the border of sovereignty and the obligations of our institutions towards their people. Police cooperation has long been within the scope of EU policy, and is the focus of the 2005 Hague Programme on the development of an area of freedom, security and justice. Market integration in the EU has now been enhanced by a Common European Defence and Security Policy. The military is no longer outside the scope of EU law and policy. At the same time, the borders of sovereignty among the Member States are increasingly common – intra Member State borders are no longer the place of control and protection against threat. Instead it is the common external border which is the focus of attention. But this common external border has also been the subject of dramatic change. In 2004 ten new Member States joined the EU enlarging the space very considerably. Further enlargement to Bulgaria, Romania and Turkey are envisaged in the near future.

Another Europe is also present in any discussion of the legality of actions by the state: that of the European Convention on Human Rights. The European Court of Human Rights has begun to refer to the convention, to which its interpretation is entrusted, as an instrument of European public order. The duty of the state to protect its people both within and outside the borders of sovereignty and the means which the state may reasonably use to do so are questions which are arising with ever greater frequency before the European Court of Human Rights. A series of cases, primarily against Turkey in the 1990s, has established beyond question the duty of the state to investigate fully allegations of extrajudicial killing and torture within its borders. A newer series of cases which have come before the Court have challenged the limitation of the duty of the state to investigation within its borders, suggesting also a duty which may extend to the actions of its agents outside its borders.

The engagement of a number of European states in military action in Iraq from 2003 onwards in support of the US invasion there has brought fresh challenges to the question of legality and action abroad. In this series of reports, we will look only at one aspect, the treatment of acts by members of the military which cause death to civilians in Iraq. In three Member States criminal charges have been laid in respect of such acts – the Netherlands, Denmark and the UK. The shadows of both the EU and the European Convention on Human Rights are evident in these cases – providing the background to what appears to be a changing dynamic to the concepts of responsibility and protection. It is our intention that by examining the specific cases and their legal framework we will contribute to a better understanding of the relationship of the internal and external in law in Europe.

Elspeth Guild
Professor of European Migration Law
Radboud University, Nijmegen
August 2005

Contents

Abbreviations

ANP	Algemeen Nederlands Persbureau (Dutch Press Agency)
CDS	Chef Defensie Staf (Chief of the Staff of Defence)
ECHR	European Convention on Human Rights
FDS	Field Dressing Station, medical personnel
Gw	Grondwet (Constitution)
MC	Military Chamber
MCP	Main Command Post
NATO	North Atlantic Treaty Organisation
PRR	Personal Role Radio
QRF	Quick Reaction Force
ROE	Rules of Engagement
SC	Security Council
SFIR	Stabilisation Force Iraq
SFOR	Stabilisation Force
UK	United Kingdom
UN	United Nations
UNAMIR	United Nations Assistance Mission for Rwanda
US	United States
WIM	Wet internationale misdrijven (International Crimes Act)
WMSr	Wetboek van Militair Strafrecht (Military Penal Code)
Zau	Ziekenauto (ambulance)

Introduction[1]

The face of global warfare is changing rapidly. Since the fall of the Berlin wall, which in turn led to the collapse of communism, the scope and gravity of international conflict has shifted from the perspective of two superpowers, assured of their mutually destructive capabilities, to regional, mostly ethnic conflicts in which the United Nations took on a leading role as peacekeeper, and finally, to the perhaps unavoidable unilateralism of the United States in response to the terrorist attacks of September 11, 2001.

Historically, sovereign states have claimed monopoly of the rightful exercise of violence. This claim can be regarded both in view of interstate-violence and the law of armed conflict, as well as in regard to the use of violence by any citizen of the state against any other.

In the changing global theatre, the legal and philosophical aspects of this monopoly of violence change accordingly. War is no longer defined as an armed conflict between two or more sovereign nations, preceded by an official declaration of a state of war; not since World War II has the only remaining superpower in the world, the United States, officially declared a state of war against another nation. The justification of the use of force is no longer sought in the legal doctrine of the *ius ad bellum*.

After a 'wave' of peacekeeping missions in the early 1990s, the shortcomings of the new philosophies on the use of violence in international conflict became painfully clear. The peace keeping missions in Somalia, Rwanda and Bosnia are now considered at least to some extent failures from both political and military perspective. Studies and evaluations of these interventions all speak of inadequate mandates, unspecific military objectives, and incapacitating limitations on the use of force.

The authorization of the United Nations Security Council to intervene on behalf of world peace, turned out to be too restricted an authorization to achieve the political and military goals derived from a desire to maintain world peace.

The lessons learned from aforementioned missions led UN Member States to become hesitant to commit themselves to peacekeeping missions around the world.

The terrorist attacks of September 11, 2001, have once again changed the face of global combat. The United States' intrusion in Iraq was not in any way approved by the UN Security Council, nor can the intrusion be considered as rightfully based on the inherent right to self-defence embedded in the United Nations' Charter, Article 51. Nevertheless, a coalition of countries led by the US conquered and occupied the state of Iraq, instated a provisional authority, and held the conquered territory for over a year and a half until the elections of last January when a new sovereign government was chosen by the Iraqis. Though the 'occupation' of Iraq was confirmed by a Security Council resolution two months after the invasion, it can no longer be held that the United Nations hold the monopoly on rightful violence or on the justification of armed conflict on a global level.

---

1 All translations are from the authors, who would like to thank Marianne Dieben for her advice and help with the translation.

The justification of the use of force is passed down and limited accordingly from the almost abstract level of nations to the more tangible level of the individual soldier entrusted with military duties. It goes without saying that any number of complications may occur when the authorization to use force is passed down from state to individual. In light of the justification of the use of force, it is then when the dilemma occurs which is referred to as the 'Arendt'-dilemma[2] by the Bureau for Ethics and Armed Force.

The responsibility for the use of force lies with some democratically elected body in any given democratic society; the armed forces are an instrument of policy made by this body. When the justification for the use of force is passed down along the chain of command, political leaders remain responsible; therefore they will define the circumstances under which they allow for the use of force. The unique perspective of the individual, however, might lead to a different assessment of what is justified based on such circumstances. A soldier now faces the dilemma of following procedure, or breaking the rules, both of which may prove to be unjustifiable.[3]

This matter becomes even more pressing in the new information age, in which the impact and ramifications of most military actions are brought to the attention of the public at large by different forms of media. Infamous incidents such as the My Lai incident live on in the collective consciousness of the American people partly because the incident was covered so extensively by the media. Technology enables society to spread news and information faster and more efficiently than ever before in human history, and this so-called 'CNN-effect' puts even more stress on the mechanisms of responsibility described above. The justification of violence is taken into the court of public opinion on a daily basis, a court that does not necessarily reach an impartial verdict. Politicians, in reaction, have become even less willing to assume responsibility for military failures or unjustifiable decisions by those in the lower ranks of the military machinery. The Arendt-dilemma arises out of this complex process.

From the monopoly of violence springs the criminal charge; in a way the two relate to one another as light relates to darkness. If violence is unjustifiable because it stems in no way from a nation's monopoly to use force, a criminal charge will be pressed against the perpetrator. If the author of the use of force is not to blame, however, the violence was in some way justifiable, either because force was used in self-defence, or because violence was used in accordance with the monopoly.

The case against Eric O., a soldier stationed in Iraq during the second Gulf War, is a criminal case; it addresses all the legal issues described in this introduction; it is the case of a soldier charged with unauthorized use of force.

The case stirred up great debate among politicians about the mandate given to soldiers, the role of criminal law in these matters and the responsibility of political leaders. In this essay the case will be reviewed from a factual, legal and political point of view. Main points of attention will be the way in which the justification of the use of force is transferred from the top to the bottom of a military organization, and how a soldier's actions should be weighed in a criminal case.

---

2 Named after Hannah Arendt (1906-1975), German philosopher.

3 The dilemma is described on p. 234 in A.H.M. van Iersel and Th. A. van Baarda (red.), *Militaire Ethiek: morele dilemma's van militairen in theorie en praktijk,* Bureau voor Ethiek en Krijgsmacht in opdracht van de Staatssecretaris van Defensie, 2002.

Part I – Facts

'When studying step 1 of [the Dutch military instructions], one has to ask instantly: which facts do I describe? Is it possible, in the emotionally charged and frustrating context of war to still portray the facts accurately? Is not the first victim of war the truth? Is not the perception of the facts constantly, but especially during a time of war, tainted by our beliefs, emotions and frustrations and our – possibly predisposed – values?'[1]

'The first casualty when war comes is truth'.[2]

1. Introduction

To select the facts in any criminal case, to set the perimeter of the case, it is essential to determine the boundaries within which the validity of legal arguments is examined. A thorough explanation of the facts is therefore an essential part of any legal essay.

In the case of Eric O., it is hard to determine whether or not the facts presented sufficiently disclose the events as they occurred and led to the prosecution of Eric O. In any case relating to national security in one way or another, the disclosure of facts might not be in the best interest of the common good. The information necessary to accurately judge the merits of the case might not have been made available to the public.

In the case of Eric O. this situation is further complicated by the great interest the media has taken in this case. Reports on the events as they took place may not have been accurate or objective.

A third complication is the fact that at least at two occasions, documents that were to some extent classified, were leaked to the media and disclosed to the public. This has sparked outrage among government officials as well as citizens, leading some to believe that a fair trial of Eric O. would be impossible in the light of the information available to all.

A proper selection of the facts is therefore limited to those facts that are necessary to get a basic grasp of the legal issues pertaining to the case. It is beyond the scope of this essay to determine or examine the validity of the facts.

To fully understand the context from which Eric O.'s case originated, it is necessary to start with a description of the events that led to the involvement of the Netherlands in Iraq; the legitimacy of the use of force does not originate from the individual.

To assess the legality of Eric O.'s use of force, it is necessary to understand the definition of the mandate set by the Dutch government. The Marchal-case, which is briefly discussed in the second part of the essay, illustrates the importance of the mandate given to the military apparatus as a whole, when an individual criminal case is brought against someone constituting a part of that apparatus. It is particularly important to get a thorough understanding of the objectives set by the government as well as the motives driving the government. Only in light of such

---

1 Van Iersel and Van Baarda (red.), *a.w.*, p. 314.
2 Hiram Warren Johnson (1866-1945), American statesman.

an understanding, the actions of an individual, acting on behalf or as an instrument of the government, can be considered in accordance with or in violation of the law.

Finally, this part of the essay will cite the most relevant sources on the incident involving Eric O.'s use of force. These sources will paint an image of the incident that will be accurate at least to some extent. Only when the facts have been presented thoroughly enough, we may start to take a look at some legal issues.

2. Events Leading to the Dutch Participation in the War in Iraq

In September 2002, intelligence agencies of both the United States and the United Kingdom publish dossiers accusing Iraq of concealed efforts to produce weapons of mass destruction. In the months following the publications, both nations threaten to take military action against Iraq if it does not cease the production of such weapons and allow for renewed inspections by UN-inspectors. Finally in November, a Security Council resolution is passed (no. 1441), speaking of 'a last chance' for Iraq to comply with UN-regulations.

In the months following the resolution, the US and the UK repeat their accusations against Iraq, and on February 2, 2003, both nations set a six week ultimatum for Iraq to comply with Resolution 1441.

On March 5, 2003, a resolution that would authorize military use of force by the Security Council, is voted down. On March 20, the US and UK commence military operations against Iraq nonetheless. This unilateral invasion sparked debate and protest around the world. The legitimacy of the invasion was debated intensely during the first days and weeks of the invasion, but even more so when the weapons of mass destruction that were supposedly at Saddam Hussein's disposal, could not be found. Van Genugten writes:

> 'The casuistry that is developing here – think of the Kurdish areas in Northern-Iraq in the beginning of the nineties, Rwanda 1994, Kosovo 1999 – offers some insight in what is and what is not allowed, what should and should not be done, put more carefully: what potentially would be allowed and should be done, to prevent dealing with a major humanitarian crisis with only a legal answer. It is clear however that the American intervention in Iraq cannot be regarded part of this doctrine, starting with the great division in the Security Council – not a clear majority (15 minus 1 or something similar) but rather split evenly at best, and this only after disproportionate pressure by the US on a number of weaker Security Council members, the use of disproportionate force, etc. Not to mention the fact that the official legitimacy of the invasion was sought in the removal of Saddam Hussein, violator of human rights, only after the start of the invasion, when doing so proved efficient and the real grounds for the invasion – the availability and willingness to use weapons of mass destruction – turned out to be increasingly problematic, not even mentioning the exit strategy (point six on my list).'[3]

The war officially lasts until May 1, 2003, when President Bush declares all major combat operations to have ended. The US then calls for the formation of an international stabilization force

---

3 W.J.M. van Genugten, De oorlog in Irak als bijdrage aan het hervormingsdebat binnen de VN, *Militair Rechtelijk Tijdschrift* 2004, afl. 5, p. 186.

in Iraq, formed out of the 'coalition of the willing'. On May 23, Security Council Resolution 1481 is passed, calling upon Member States to contribute to the stability and security in Iraq.

In the opinion of some, diplomatic ties are restored by Resolution 1481 (at least to some extent). No longer is the military action in Iraq a unilateral intervention by one or two nations without the authorization of the Security Council. In a way, all military activities in Iraq now lack the characteristics of war; the rightfulness of the invasion by US/UK forces no longer affects the rightfulness of future military activity by other nations.

It is doubtful, however, if Resolution 1481 can be regarded without taking into account the failure to pass a resolution that would have approved military action before the invasion. The fact that the US and UK went along without such authorization, confronted the UN with a 'fait accompli'; nonetheless several nations comply with the request of Resolution 1483. Among these nations is the Netherlands.

3. The Commitment of Dutch Troops to Iraq

3.1. The Applicable Legal Framework ('Toetsingskader')

It is necessary to briefly describe the relation between the government and Parliament in Dutch constitutional law when it comes to the deployment of armed forces. This will give a better understanding of the sources used in this part of the essay.

Based on the relevant paragraphs in the Dutch Constitution, the applicable legal framework (Toetsingskader) can be seen as a framework implementing the responsibilities attributed to the government by these paragraphs, among which ranks highly the obligation to inform Parliament of any decision to deploy troops when the necessity of such a deployment derives from the international rule of law, to which the government is legally committed by the Constitution (Article 100 Gw).

The legal framework defines the way in which Parliament is informed of such decisions, as well as a number of subjects that need to be addressed by the government when Parliament is informed. Among these subjects are safety issues, environmental circumstances, legal mandate, and military objectives. Because of the requirements of this legal framework, the decision of the government to deploy troops is communicated to Parliament in a considerably transparent way.

The analysis of the decisions of the Dutch government to commit troops to Iraq will be based on the information made available to Parliament, based on the legal framework.

3.2. The Decision of June 6, 2003

Less than three weeks after Resolution 1481 is passed by the Security Council, the Council of Minsters decides on June 6, 2003, to send a battalion of troops to the southern part of Iraq; the battalion will consist of approximately 1,100 military troops including personnel. It will contribute to the multinational stabilization force for an initial period of six months.

Dutch troops will be deployed in the province of Al-Muthanna, in the southern sector of Iraq, under British control.[4]

Grounds for Participation

The government states, that in participating in the operation in Iraq, it responds to the appeal made in Resolution 1483 of the Security Council. In their joint announcement to Parliament, the Ministers of Defence and Foreign Affairs state:

> 'In the opinion of the government, UN Security Council Resolution 1483 constitutes [...] the political and legal basis for participation in the stabilization force [...]'[5]

In response to questions from Parliament, the government confirms this view.[6] The government refers to the relevant paragraphs no. 1 and 26 of the Resolution, which state:

> 'welcoming further the willingness of Member States to contribute to stability and security in Iraq by contributing personnel, equipment, and other resources under the Authority,
> [...]
> 1. *Appeals* to Member States and concerned organizations to assist the people of Iraq in their efforts to reform their institutions and rebuild their country, and to contribute to conditions of stability and security in Iraq in accordance with this resolution
> [...]
> 26. *Calls upon* Member States and international and regional organizations to contribute to the implementation of this resolution'.

Aside from Resolution 1483, the government believes that the military mandate is also based on the so-called 'concept of operations' of the United Kingdom. The relationship between the resolution and the concept of operations is described by the government in response to parliamentary questions:

> 'The SC resolution gives the legal and political framework within which the operation shall be executed. The concept of operations then determines how to deal with it.'[7]

Overall, the government attaches a great deal of value to the Security Council resolution. The concept of operations between the Dutch government and the UK can be seen as a military agreement on more specific strategic and military matters.

As has been mentioned before, the doctrine on the justification of war (the so called *ius ad bellum*) has changed immensely since the Second World War. It can be argued that no legality can directly be derived from a resolution dealing with the aftermath of a war, which had no explicit legal basis in international law. However, the grounds for intervention should not be confused with the legitimacy of such an intervention. Whether or not Resolution 1483 serves as

4 TK 23432 nr. 116, June 6, 2003.
5 TK 23432 nr. 116 , June 6, 2003.
6 TK 23432, nr. 117, June 18, 2003.
7 *Ibid.*

sufficient basis from the perspective of international law, it nonetheless forms the legal ground for the Dutch presence in Iraq.

Objectives

The government clearly formulates its objectives in Iraq: the Dutch are to assist in the reconstruction of Iraq through the creation of a safe and stable environment. The Netherlands will provide a supporting contribution to the 'Authority' for a number of specific tasks; among those tasks are the maintaining of security and stability, and the enabling of activities of humanitarian organizations.[8]

With regard to the way in which Dutch troops may take action, the government states:

> 'The stabilization force will support rather than replace Iraqi structures. [...] The intention is not to place emphasis on military presence.'[9]

Legal Status of the Dutch Military Presence in Iraq

The unilateral intervention of the UK and US and the passing of Resolution 1483 after the removal of Saddam Hussein's government from office, leads to a noteworthy difference between the legal status of 'occupying nation' that is assigned to the UK and US by Resolution 1483, and the status of all other nations as non-occupying nations.

The Dutch government refers to the preamble of Resolution 1483 in which this distinction is made:

> '*Noting* the letter of 8 May 2003 for the Permanent Representatives of the United States of America and the United Kingdom of Great Britain and Northern Ireland [...] and recognizing the specific authorities, responsibilities and obligations under applicable international law of these states as occupying powers under unified command (the 'Authority'), ...
>
> *Noting further* that other States that are not occupying powers are working now or in the future may work under the Authority, ...'

In relation with the objectives the government has set for the Dutch forces in Iraq, it is clear that their presence is not to be compared to the presence of American or British troops. The Dutch government clearly intends for Dutch troops to take on a supporting role rather than a leading one.

Accordingly, the tasks and duties of the Dutch soldier will differ from those of his American or British counterpart. Though one should only cautiously draw conclusions from such differences, one could argue that the Dutch soldier would be more restricted in the use of force than the American or British soldier. Though at this stage, no comparison is yet being made between the responsibilities of a police officer and those of a soldier, the incident involving Eric O. will give rise to numerous questions relating to the similarities and differences between the use of force by a police officer and the use of force by a soldier.

8 TK 23432, nr. 116, June 6, 2003.
9 *Ibid.*

Rules of Engagement
The authorization to use force, as well as the limitations surrounding the use of force, are translated to a more operational level in a set of rules generally called the Rules of Engagement. Such a set of rules is drafted to translate the mandate, on which military action is based, to the level of more specific directives that may, for example, authorize the use of laser-guided weapon systems or exclude the use of anti-personnel mines.

Traditionally, the Rules of Engagement also describe when deadly force can be used by individual military personnel. The legal aspects of the rules of engagement will be discussed in part II of the essay.

The Rules of Engagement (ROE) are usually adopted from the so called 'lead nation' that has the general command for a military operation or military sector. The southern part of Iraq, including the Al-Muthanna province, was under British rule in the summer of 2003. This implied that Dutch forces would adopt the ROE set by British command.

Limitations on the ROE that would apply to Dutch soldiers only, can be set forth by additional directives issued to all soldiers. The Dutch so-called 'Instructions on the use of force' (*Geweldsinstructie*) are an example of such a directive.

The government, in its communication with Parliament, states:

> 'that these (ROE) shall be robust, meaning amongst other things that there will be extensive authorization for 'force protection', as well as the creation of a safe and stable environment. Based upon this, the government considers the ROE to provide for sufficient possibilities to execute the tasks in the event of hostilities or disturbances.'[10]

In rebuttal to questions asked by Parliament, the government states:

> 'To ensure this, regulations have been adopted that define the circumstance under which it is allowed to proceed to the use of force in self-defence or in accordance with the execution of the mission.'[11]

Security Risks and Safety Issues pertaining to the Stabilization Force
The government describes the situation in the southern part of Iraq as 'reasonably safe', particularly when compared to the situation in Baghdad and the central part of the country.

However, the government states that the fact should be taken into consideration, that wherever a situation of relative peace exists, that situation can worsen unexpectedly. Factors relating to the security of the stabilization force in general, are, among others, the attitude of the local population towards the stabilization force, possible remains of the old regime under Saddam Hussein, and the way in which different political and religious fractions will interact.

3.3. The Decision of November 28, 2003

The decision to send troops to Iraq set a six-month term on the presence of the troops in Iraq. Accordingly, a longer stay for the troops would require a decision to extend the term.

---

10 TK 23432, nr. 116, June 6, 2003.
11 TK 23432, nr. 117, June 18, 2003.

Such a decision was reached on November 28th. Parliament was informed shortly after in compliance with the legal framework.

The government decided to keep the Dutch troops in Iraq for an additional six months. In addition, the government dispatched an extra reconnaissance unit consisting of 70 soldiers as well as a fourth Chinook helicopter to support the troops already present in Iraq.

The shooting incident involving Eric O. took place during this second term of the Dutch presence in Iraq.

Grounds for the Extension

During the initial six months, Resolution 1511 was passed by the Security Council, confirming and broadening the mandate set forth by Resolution 1483. The government's view remains to be that Resolution 1483 is the legal and political mandate on which participation is based, but additionally states that Resolution 1511, adopted on October 16, 2003, reinforces this mandate.

The government states that the mandate shall end,

> 'the moment the political process, described in Resolution 1511, is completed'.[12]

It is the government's belief that the unanimous adoption of Resolution 1511 does not change the legal grounds for participation:

> 'The existing structures in Iraq, the ways of government or the role of the Authority. [...] The Security Council does, however, explicitly authorize the presence of a multinational military force under united command, consisting of all military units of both occupying powers and other nations.'[13]

Aside from Resolutions 1483 and 1511, the military mission of the battalion is also based on the 'mission as it is defined in the 'memorandum of understanding' concluded between the United Kingdom and the participating countries in the British controlled division sector'.[14]

Objectives

The government considers it the task of the multinational force to secure safety and stability, the conditions for the completion of the political and economic reconstruction process.[15] The government refers to Resolution 1511. Paragraph 13 of this resolution states:

> '13. Determines that the provision of security and stability is essential to the successful completion of the political process as outlined in paragraph 7 above and to the ability of the United Nations to contribute effectively to that process and the implementation of Resolution 1483 (2003), and authorizes a multinational force under unified command to take all necessary measures to contribute to the maintenance of security and stability in Iraq, including for the purpose of ensuring necessary conditions for the implementation of the time-table and programme as well as to contribute to the security of the United Na-

12 TK 23432, nr. 135, November 28, 2003.

13 *Ibid.*

14 TK 23432, nr. 135, November 28, 2003.

15 *Ibid.*

tions Assistance Mission for Iraq, the Governing Council of Iraq and other institutions of the Iraqi interim administration, and key humanitarian and economic infrastructure.'

ROE

With regard to the ROE, the government states to Parliament:

> 'During the past period, no problems have arisen nor have any developments taken place with regard to the Instructions on the use of force. The current Instructions on the use of force are clear and practicable.'[16]

The applicable Dutch Instructions on the use of force will remain to be adopted from the 'lead nation', the United Kingdom. The government reiterates that this directive is 'robust'.[17] In reply to the decision to extend the presence of Dutch troops, parliamentary commissions on Foreign Affairs and Defence ask the government if the adjustment of the so-called threat analysis from 'low' to 'average' will lead to operational changes and if the adjustment will in any way affect the Instructions on the use of force. The government answers that it does not.[18]

Security Risks and Safety Issues

The government states that the situation in Iraq has deteriorated. The threat analysis concerning attacks and acts of terrorism is adjusted by the government. Though the first signals of recovery of a local structure in the province of Al-Muthanna are positive, a climate could develop that would facilitate crime and sabotage.[19]

3.4. The Decision of June 11, 2004

There is a third decision of some importance to Eric O.'s criminal case, namely the decision taken after the shooting incident has taken place. Despite the political uproar that was caused by the incident and its significant aftermath, the government extends the stay of troops in Iraq with another eight months on June 11.

Grounds for Extension

The government still considers the presence of Dutch troops essential to the creation of stability and security in Iraq; the government attaches great value to the request by Prime Minister Allawi on behalf of the Iraqi interim government, to continue the presence of the multinational military force in Iraq.[20]

Rules of Engagement

Despite the incident involving Eric O., the Rules of Engagement remain unchanged. The government states that the question whether the ROE needs to be changed, should be answered by

16 *Ibid.*
17 *Ibid.*
18 TK 23432, nr. 136, December 8, 2003.
19 TK 23432, nr. 135, November 28, 2003.
20 TK 23432, nr. 164, June 11, 2004.

the lead nation.[21] Whether or not that statement relates in some way to the incident involving Eric O., is not specified.

Answering questions from Parliament, the government reiterates its statement that the ROE requires no adaptation.[22]

Security Issues and Safety Risk

The government states that a number of incidents involving Dutch military have occurred over time in the province of Al-Muthanna. Such incidents primarily took place near check points of local security organizations and Dutch troops. Also, the Dutch bases were fired upon a number of times with mortar shells. On May 10, 2004, a Dutch soldier was killed during an attack.[23]

4. The Shooting Incident

The Eric O. incident takes place on December 27, 2003.

Letter of the Minister of Defence to Parliament

The Minister of Defence, Mr Kamp, describes the incident in his letter of January 6, 2004, to Parliament:

> 'During a shooting incident in the province of Al-Muthanna in Iraq on December 27th, an Iraqi man was fatally wounded. By order of the public prosecution service, the Military Police have opened an investigation of the incident. The Military Police, under the authority of the public prosecution service, thoroughly investigates cases in which there is reasonable suspicion a criminal offence has been committed. The public prosecution service has deemed the incident of December 27th, 2003 in Iraq, cause for a criminal investigation.
> [...]
> With reference to the incident, I have had verified whether the Instructions on the use of force suffice and, based on information available, I have concluded that such is unabatedly the case.'[24]

Letter of the Procurator General to the Heads of the Public Prosecutor Offices

On January 15, 2004, the Procurator General of the public prosecution service, Mr De Wijkerslooth, writes to the heads of the public prosecutor offices, in a confidential letter:

> 'On December 27th, a member of the Quick Reaction Force (QRF) of the Dutch forces in Iraq killed an Iraqi. This happened while the Quick Reaction Force had come to assist during the securing of an army container that had fallen off a truck. The container contained steel cases.
> The soldier involved had fired at a group of Iraqis that had taken on a provocative attitude, from a distance of approximately 100 meters. The soldier involved had first fired a

21 *Ibid.*
22 TK 23432, nr. 165, June 21, 2004.
23 TK 23432, nr. 164, June 11, 2004.
24 TK 23432, nr. 145, January 6, 2004.

warning shot in the air and had then fired a second warning shot in the ground to the left of the group. An Iraqi standing in the middle of the group, was hit in the back.
The incident occurred at 13.55 local time. It was not reported to the Military Police by the navy until 16.20. Because of the lateness of the report to the Military Police, the bodily remains of the victim could not be examined. The body had already been buried at a sacred cemetery.
However, the body had been examined by a local physician. That same night, the Military Police reported the case to the public prosecutor in Arnhem. The question was raised whether the use of force had been proportional.
The first statements of the members of the QRF heard as witnesses showed that the situation had not been experienced as threatening. From American side came a surprised reaction to the shooting.'[25]

Press Report ANP, December 28, 2003

'Last Saturday, Dutch soldiers in Iraq have driven away a group of approximately seventy Iraqis attempting to plunder a container. Dutch soldiers fired rounds during the incident. An Iraqi was injured and died in a hospital later, presumably due to the rifle fire.
This has been reported by a spokesperson for the Ministry of Defence on Sunday. There were no casualties among Dutch soldiers. The incident took place in the province of Al Muthanna, on the main road between the cities of Al Khidr and As Samawah, where the Dutch soldiers are stationed.
[...]
According to the Ministry of Defence, the container involved had fallen off a truck. The unarmed convoy, consisting of several trucks, had already moved on. Iraqis then tried to plunder the container, until several Dutch soldiers arrived on the scene. According to the Ministry of Defence, warning shots were fired because the number of plunderers was considerable and they had taken on an obtrusive attitude. The Military Police is investigating the incident.'[26]

Closing Speech of the Public Prosecutor[27]

The closing speech of the public prosecutor addresses a number of witness testimonies. They describe in detail the situation as described by the witnesses.

The closing speech, however, cannot be considered an objective source of information. Also, a number of witnesses have changed or withdrawn their testimonies before or during the trial.

Nonetheless, certain witness statements shed a different light on the case, regardless of the fact that they were presented to the court by the prosecution.

Sergeant P., 23rd Infantry Company, stationed at Al Khidr, accidentally passes the site between quarter past nine and half past nine with his rifle company (8 people), when the Americans are trying to get the semi-trailer back on the road (p. 678). The semi-trailer is bent and total loss. The Americans leave the semi-trailer and the container.

---

25 Letter by mr. J.M. De Wijkerslooth, voorzitter van het College van procureurs-generaal, aan De hoofden van de parketten, e.a., confidential letter of January 15, 2004.

26 December 28, 2003, '*Nederlanders verjagen Iraakse plunderaars*', Bergsma Raven, Den Haag/As Samawah (ANP).

27 Containing the demand that a penalty be imposed.

[...]
It is agreed that the group of P. will be relieved by the companies-QRF (Quick Reaction Force) of the 23rd Infantry Company, for temporary security, until the moment of salvage.
[...]
The battalions QRF arrive at approximately 12.46 hour (MCP log 1097) with two Patria's and consists of 16 people, among which 4 soldiers of the FDS (Field Dressing Station, medical personnel) and an under officer and a corporal of the genie. Suspect is the commander of this QRF.
It is then that the American convoy with the prefabs wants to pass the salvage area. The road is blocked by the two Patria's. The Patri Zau (ziekenauto, 'ambulance') blocks the road in the direction of Al Khidr and the QRF Patria blocks the road in the direction of As Samawah. At 13.05, the start of the salvaging is reported over the radio of the 23e (Radiolog 23rd).
[...]

2.1 Witnesses about the situation at the scene
Sergeant P. (678) states:
[...]
Meanwhile Iraqis had arrived. They were particularly interested in the semi-trailer. When P. had pushed the semi-trailer further into the terrain, the Iraqis saw this as a sign that it was their turn now. They started stripping the semi-loader. P. allowed them to have the parts. The semi-trailer was useless anyway and was not to be salvaged.
When a quarrel erupted among the locals and hindrance was caused to traffic subsequently, he took action and eventually fired in the air twice. That helped. Everyone disappeared into the terrain to the side. The situation was not threatening. According to P. 'they don't care about you, but about your stuff'. He testifies that the shots were therefore not fired because he considered the situation dangerous, but to draw attention and make something clear (679).
(689) (Corporal) T. tells him about the contents of the container, after which suspect orders both sides of the road closed to create space for the salvaging. At that moment an American convoy of prefabs comes from the direction of Al Khidr. T. sees it coming and brings it to the attention of suspect.
[...]
The convoy comes to a halt. This creates a situation in which people from the area aside the road actually start plundering the goods of the prefabs or threaten to do so. T. allows marine C. to fire warning shots. C. fires in the air seven times and T. himself fires three times, which helps: the people flee into the side terrain. (682)
Corporal R. (486), successive commander of the battalions QRF, testifies: '[...] At a certain moment I have armed my rifle to show that it had to stop now. I did not do this for safety. I was annoyed. I was tired of having to come back every time and I hoped that arming my weapon would impress more.'
[...]

2.3 Testimony and experience sergeant-major H.
The testimony of sergeant-major H. of the 23rd shows that a different perception exists of the behaviour of the Iraqis with regard to abandoned goods and that this behaviour even shows a pattern.

[...]

H. (781) further testifies: 'The word plundering is used in a wrong way here and in the media. The locals strip the vehicles that are abandoned because they can use the stuff. I know from my own experience that when warning shots are fired, the locals immediately disperse. I know from my own experience that these locals always sit at a certain distance from us and when they think we are leaving, they will try to see first whether there is something of their liking.'

[...]

R. says about this: 'When a vehicle in Iraq is flipped over, people will try to take everything off the vehicle and take it with them. The Dutch soldiers were busy keeping them at a distance; these people wait for their chance when the Dutch soldiers leave.

Verdict of the Military Chamber of the Arnhem District Court

On October 18, 2004, the Military Chamber of the Arnhem District Court ruled in the case. The court, regarding the facts of the case relating to the incident, found:

'suspect was ordered to salvage the container. This involved a number of aspects: securing the salvage activities, protecting the container (force property); the transport of the container, the securing of the Quick Reaction Force (QRF) (force protection).

Suspect had to accomplish this task under difficult circumstances. On arrival, there was chaos, aggravated by the blocking of the road, causing traffic jams on both sides of the salvage activities, with agitated Iraqis and an American convoy consisting of low loaders with prefabs.

The prefabs were of great interest to the Iraqis, who again and again attempted to come closer from the areas aside the road, to capture goods valuable to them off the trucks, semi-trailers, and their cargo.

The disorder was further worsened because of an American convoy of prisoners that had to cross the site of the salvage activities. Right before the incident, the convoy with prefabs started moving. The convoy was about to cross the site, but was halted, leading the first vehicle to stop in front of the Patria Zau.

Taking into account this situation, suspect did not have a sufficient number of men at his disposal for his security task, to adequately execute the salvaging mission over a 100 to 150 meter operational width.

He had to take care of the personal security of the salvors; the medical personnel could not be used for the security of his group; one marine had to stand next to him in order to maintain radio contact with the Main Command Post (MCP) through the Patria Zau, and the Zau had to be secured as well.

He therefore had only a number of men at his disposal to secure the salvaging operation as a whole.

In addition, the communication among the men was inadequate due to insufficient functioning of the Personal Role Radio (PRR).

When the container was raised on the low loader, the crane was packed and the 23rd – on the flank in the direction of Al Khidr – started preparing for departure, a crowd of approximately 100 Iraqis (divided in several groups) was present in the areas aside the road at the height of the recovery site.

When the last marine, who had kept these groups at a distance from the recovery site, walked back to the road, some Iraqis started moving in the direction of the recovery site.

Suspect then armed his weapon, visible for the approaching groups. The groups, however, continued walking. Suspect then fired a warning shot in the air. Despite this, a small part of the groups continued to walk towards the road. At that moment – the Iraqis were then approximately 75 meters removed from him, according to his testimony – suspect fired a warning shot to the left and in front of the group, into the ground. The crane operator [name] testifies that at that moment he saw sand fly up at approximately one-third of the distance between the suspect and the Iraqis. Shortly afterwards (no more than two seconds) the Iraqi was seen falling, and then immediately taken to the road by other Iraqis, close to the site of, among others, suspect. This Iraqi was severely wounded.'[28]

28 District Court Arnhem, October 18, 2004, LJN AR4029.

Part II – Law

1. Introduction

A monopoly of violence cannot exist without a criminal code that makes punishable the use of violence not in accordance with the will of the monopolist. In any society based upon the rule of law, the monopolist will only allow for the use of force if such usage will in one way or another contribute to the well-being of society as a whole. The law will reflect the means the monopolist deems necessary to achieve this well-being of society, as well as the limitations the monopolist sets on ethical or political grounds.

The monopolist is therefore the source of legality of the use of force. With an authorization to use force comes the lawfulness of such use; any criminal code will be the mirror image of the scope and nature of the monopoly.

There is one exception to this rule: in certain situations, the authorization of the monopolist to use force cannot be awaited. Such situations will call for the use of force, though no prior legality of the use of such force has been established; the law is taken into one's own hands.

As said, these situations call for immediate action; their common characteristic is that reaction by the appropriate authorities cannot be awaited. The defence of essential interests requires swift action.

The principles of law attribute legality to such actions in retrospect. Though the conduct of the perpetrator might be qualified as criminal by the applicable criminal code, the unlawfulness of his actions is annulled because similar actions would have been taken by the monopolist were he present or if his authorization were awaited.

Translated to the use of force by a soldier, two principle grounds for legal use of such force thus exist: the use of force as mandated by the society he serves, and the use of force in self-defence.

This part of the essay will examine these two grounds; it will examine the legal mandate given to the military forces in Iraq, as well as the legal significance of the mandate, and secondly, the criminal code applicable to soldiers. Furthermore, it will examine the theory of self-defence in combat environments.

2. Applicable Law

In the case against Eric O. several bodies of law apply. These bodies will be discussed from the most general, being treaties on international or European level applying to all citizens, to the most specific, being the directives in force for the armed forces stationed in Iraq.

This essay is limited to the scope of law at the level of the individual; no law will be discussed regulating warfare at the level of the military apparatus in general, like the Land War Treaty, since it has no direct relevance to the case of Eric O.; such laws might regulate the use of certain weapons systems, or battle operations.

2.1. International and European Treaties

The Geneva Conventions

The Geneva Conventions (also called the Red Cross Conventions) are four treaties drafted in 1949 in Geneva, intended to improve the treatment of the wounded and ill among the forces present on the battlefield, as well as the treatment of prisoners of war and civilian persons during a time of war. The treaties cover a wide array of acts and call for their penalization.

> 'The treaties oblige the contracting parties (including the Netherlands):
> - to make punishable by national law severe violations of the treaties, committed by anyone anywhere;
> - to make punishable by law the ordering of such violations;
> - to track down persons suspected of (punishable) violations of the treaties;
> - to try and extradite to another concerned state (if party to the treaty) apprehended persons, regardless of nationality;
> - to take action to prevent non-severe violations of the treaties (as well).
>
> The treaties define precisely which violations of the treaties are considered severe violations.
> The following acts, for example, are considered grave violations when committed against a person protected by the treaties: 'intentional manslaughter, torture or inhumane treatment (including biological testing); deliberately causing severe suffering, inflict grievous bodily harm, or causing severe damage to health'.'[1]

The Netherlands has met the obligation of making punishable by national law severe violations by enacting the International Crimes Act (*Wet Internationale Misdrijven*, WIM) in 2003, replacing the War Crimes Act (*Wet Oorlogsmisdrijven*), passed in 1952. The WIM will be discussed later.

Convention on the Prevention and Punishment of the Crime of Genocide

The Convention on Genocide was drafted in 1948 and ratified by the Netherlands in 1960. Article 2 of the treaty defines genocide:

> 'Article 2
> In the present Convention, genocide means any of the following acts committed with intent to destroy, in whole or in part, a national, ethnical, racial or religious group, as such:
> (a) Killing members of the group;
> (b) Causing serious bodily or mental harm to members of the group;
> (c) Deliberately inflicting on the group conditions of life calculated to bring about its physical destruction in whole or in part;
> (d) Imposing measures intended to prevent births within the group;
> (e) Forcibly transferring children of the group to another group.'

Article 5 of the Convention then obliges the contracting parties to make genocide punishable by their national laws.

1 G.L. Coolen, *Militair Straf- en strafprocesrecht*, 3e druk, Zwolle, W.E.J. Tjeenk Willink, 2000, p. 123.

> 'Article 5
> The Contracting Parties undertake to enact, in accordance with their respective Constitutions, the necessary legislation to give effect to the provisions of the present Convention, and, in particular, to provide effective penalties for persons guilty of genocide or any of the other acts enumerated in Article III.'

Originally, genocide was punishable under Dutch law through the Act to implement the Genocide Convention. This law was amended by the aforementioned WIM, and genocide is now punishable under the WIM.

The Convention against Torture, and Other Cruel, Inhuman or Degrading Treatment or Punishment
The Netherlands is party to the Convention against torture of 1984, obliging contracting parties to punish and prosecute torture, as defined by the Convention in Article 1:

> 'Article I
> 1. For the purposes of this Convention, the term "torture" means any act by which severe pain or suffering, whether physical or mental, is intentionally inflicted on a person for such purposes as obtaining from him or a third person information or a confession, punishing him for an act he or a third person has committed or is suspected of having committed, or intimidating or coercing him or a third person, or for any reason based on discrimination of any kind, when such pain or suffering is inflicted by or at the instigation of or with the consent or acquiescence of a public official or other person acting in an official capacity. It does not include pain or suffering arising only from, inherent in or incidental to lawful sanctions.'

Similar to the other treaties discussed is the Act to implement the Convention against Torture. This Act penalizes torture as defined by Article 1 of the Convention. Again, this law was amended by the WIM so that the WIM is now the relevant penal law.

The European Convention on Human Rights
The ECHR does not so much bind the individual, but rather binds Member States that have ratified the Convention. Article 2 of the Convention guarantees the right to life, Article 3 prohibits torture. Article 4 prohibits slavery and forced labour. According to Article 15 of the treaty, a violation of Article 2 can only be legally based on lawful acts of war; the Articles 3, 4 and 7 of the Convention can never be lawfully violated.

Based on the ECHR, the Dutch government could be convicted by the European Court on Human Rights for acts of torture, genocide, etc., but the most important difference between the European Convention and the other treaties mentioned above, is the fact that the ECHR does not penalize at the level of the individual, whereas the other treaties have led to national laws making war crimes punishable.

A perpetrator could not be convicted for violating the European Conventions; he could, however, be convicted for any violation of the WIM.

2.2. Dutch law

The Dutch Penal Code

On the national level, the most important piece of legislation is the Penal Code.

It applies to all Dutchmen, including members of the armed forces. A ruling of the Supreme Court (*Hoge Raad*) confirmed this.[2] The most important provision of the criminal code to the case of Eric O. is Article 41, which covers the concept of self-defence.

The International Crimes Act

The International Crimes Act (*Wet Internationale Misdrijven*, WIM) has been mentioned before. The law was passed in 2003, to comply with the statute for the International Criminal Court, among other reasons. The law replaced the Martial Law Act, the Act to implement the Torture Convention, and the Act to implement the Genocide Convention.

The WIM is thus a comprehensive addition to the Dutch Penal Code, giving any Dutch court jurisdiction over a number of war crimes. A criminal case can be brought to the court by the prosecution based on the WIM. Therefore, any Dutchman is punishable under the WIM for committing war crimes, regardless of the fact whether such crimes were committed within the Netherlands, and regardless of his status as either civilian or a member of the armed forces.

2.3. Military law

Military Penal Code

The Military Penal Code (*Wetboek van Militair Strafrecht*, WMSr) constitutes the main body of criminal law applicable to those who meet the definition of soldier. This definition is given in Article 60 WMSr:

> 'Article 60
> 1. A Soldier is defined as:
> 1°. One whose voluntary employment obliges him to continuing actual service, during the whole period of his employment
> 2°. All other volunteers with the armed services and the conscripts, as often and as long as they are in actual service, and also when they commit any of the crimes defined in the articles 109 and 110 of this code, when not in actual service during the time period they can be drafted for service.'

The Military Penal Code applies to anyone who meets the definition of Article 60 WMSr, whether or not crimes are committed on Dutch soil. This principle is called the 'flag principle' and is stated in Article 4 WMSr:

> 'Article 4
> The Dutch criminal code applies to the soldier, who commits any crime outside of the Netherlands.'

---

2 HR December 23, 1980, *MRT* 1981, p. 300.

The Military Penal Code can be considered an addition to the Dutch Penal Code, and it only applies to those who meet the criteria of Article 60. Contrary to the WIM, which applies to every Dutch citizen, crimes listed in the Military Penal Code cannot be committed by civilians. Jurisdiction over such crimes is given to the Military Chamber of the Arnhem District Court; they cannot be tried before a civil court (Article 3 WMSr).

Time of War/Time of Peace

A major difference between the Military Penal Code and the general Penal Code, is the fact that an aggravating factor is established when any crime listed in the Military Penal Code is committed during a time of war. The Code distinguishes between a 'time of war' and a 'time of peace'. 'Time of war' is defined by Article 87 of the Dutch Penal Code.

> 'Article 87
> -1. Enemy also includes insurgents.
> -2. War also includes civil war.
> -3. Time of war also includes a time when war is imminent. Time of war exists also when conscripts are drafted into extraordinary service and while they are extraordinarily in actual service.'

Several authors have described this distinction as meaningless.

> 'Time of war is a completely outdated concept. Wars as defined by international law only rarely occur nowadays. For example, the Netherlands was not at war with Iraq during the Gulf war (in 1991) and so a time of war was non-existent – since an announcement as defined by article 71 WMSr was not issued.
> It is indeed irrelevant whether a time of war existed when a criminal act was committed. It is only relevant whether the crime was committed under circumstances that justify a more severe punishment. Therefore, the term 'time of war' in the Military Penal Code, could better be replaced by the term 'under operational circumstances'.'[3]

A ruling by the Military Chamber on March 1, 2004, in a case against two soldiers who had fallen asleep at their post, also illustrates that the term 'time of war' is not relevant to Eric O.'s criminal case. The Chamber found that a time of war did not exist during the military operations in Iraq:

> 'The Military Chamber finds that no instance of war occurred, considering that a war as defined by international law, noting Article 87 of the Dutch Penal Code and Article 96 of the Constitution, did not occur.
> With regard to the question whether actual war circumstances exist, the Military Chamber finds that the documents presented by the public prosecutor (among others UN-Resolution 1483, the letter of June 6th, 2003 of the Ministers of Foreign Affairs and Defence, Parliamentary publications) cannot lead to the conclusion that actual war circumstances were present when the crime was committed.

---

3 Coolen 2000, *a.w.*, p. 98.

> The Military Chamber notes that the participation in peace and security operations in an international context cannot simply be classified as war or as circumstances of war.
> [...]
> The Military Chamber therefore finds the element 'in time of war' not lawfully proven. In addition, the Military Chamber notes that the current terminology in the Military Penal Code no longer sufficiently relates to the changing operational circumstances under which the armed forces have to perform their international tasks.'[4]

2.4. Rules of Engagement/Instructions on the Use of Force/Service Regulations

The ROE are a set of rules drafted by strategic command, relating to operational aspects of a given mission.

> 'Depending upon one's perspective, Rules of Engagement (ROE) are the means by which restrictions are placed upon – or authorization is granted for – the use of force by military personnel.'[5]

The ROE are generally classified. In the Eric O. case, the initial court ruled on their legal status:

> 'In general, the Military Chamber finds that both the Aide-Mémoire and the Instructions on the use of force are service regulations. They contain not only instructions, but also orders and prohibitions; they are of general purport, and also, for that matter, fall under the definition and requirements of a service regulation set by Article 135 Military Penal Code. The Rules of Engagement (ROE) are indeed of a different nature.'[6]

The ruling on appeal qualifies the ROE differently:

> 'b5. The court finds that the ROE meet the demands set by Article 135 of the Military Penal Code for a service regulation.'[7]

This status is relevant in relation to Article 136 WMSr, which penalizes a violation of such a service regulation, when danger or death is caused. The charges brought against Eric O. were based on this article of the Military Penal Code, thus making the qualification of the ROE and the Instructions on the use of force relevant. Eric O.'s counsel had argued that since the ROE and the Instructions on the use of force were not service regulations, no service regulation was violated by Eric O. The ruling denies the ROE the status of a service regulation as defined by the Military Penal Code.

As said, the ROE are normally adopted from the lead nation. As a result, they are of an international character. The Instructions on the use of force are a service regulation applying only to Dutch soldiers; as the Military Chamber confirms, it is a service regulation, contrary to the ROE; therefore, the Dutch Military Penal Code applies to possible violations.

---

4 Rechtbank Arnhem, March 1, 2004, *NJ* 2004/206.

5 A.S. Paphiti UK A, Rules of Engagement within multinational land operations, *Militair Rechtelijk Tijdschrift*, nr. 1, 1996, p. 1.

6 District Court Arnhem, October 18, 2004, LJN AR4029.

7 Court of Justice Arnhem, May 4, 2005, LJN AT4988.

The ruling on appeal does qualify the ROE as a service regulation covered by the Dutch Penal Code. Despite its international nature, the Court finds that it clearly meets the definition of a service regulation set by the Military Penal Code. This is a major difference between the initial ruling and the ruling on appeal.

The difference between the ROE and de Instructions on the use of force is relevant when it comes to the authorization of the use of force, see Part III.

3. Charges Brought Against Eric O.

On July 13, 2004, the public prosecution service decides to prosecute Eric O. on grounds that he violated service regulations leading to a casualty, as penalized by Article 136 of the Military Penal Code.

> 'The public prosecution service in Arnhem has decided to prosecute suspect in the case regarding the shooting incident of December 27th, 2003.
> Suspect is charged with violation of service regulations applicable to Dutch soldiers in Iraq, by firing a shot in the direction of a group of Iraqis. According to the public prosecution service, this resulted in the killing of one and doing so posed a threat to the life of others.
> This is a military offence penalized by the Military Penal Code (Article 136 WMSr).
> Subsidiary, suspect is charged with death caused by negligent behaviour.
> The public prosecution service is planning to bring the case before the Military Chamber of the Arnhem District Court on September 27th, 2004.'[8]

The nature of this charge limits the case to the question whether service regulations were disobeyed by Eric O., causing either death or danger. If such a violation would have taken place, he could then be convicted on that ground.

The nature of the charge, as well as the nature of the Dutch penal system, also limits the case because if no such violation is proven, no conviction can follow.

4. The Use of Force

This limits the legal aspects of the case to two questions: first, whether Eric O. violated service regulations, and second, if such a violation could be justified on the ground that Eric O. acted in self-defence. This is in accordance with what has been said before: violence is lawful either when mandated by the monopolist, or when necessary in self-defence.

These two grounds for the legal use of force are recognized by legal doctrine. Coolen writes:

> 'Soldiers are also allowed to and often obliged to use force, not only in time of war but also in peace time. This stems from the tasks attributed to the armed forces by the consti-

8 Press report District Court Arnhem, July 13, 2004.

tution. These (...) tasks include (as stated in Article 97 of the Constitution): the defence and protection of the interests of the Kingdom and the promotion of the international rule of law.'[9]

On self-defence, he writes:

> 'The fact that service regulations are in force during a peacekeeping operation, does not imply that use of force is necessarily prohibited when not in accordance with such regulations. The use of force is legitimate if necessary in the context of self-defence, even without such service regulations.
> [...]
> Article 41 of the Penal code applies to the Dutch soldier acting in self-defence – circumventing the applicable Instructions on the use of force.[10]

Major-General Van Diepenbrugge summarizes:

> 'In principle however, the use of force is prohibited during a peace keeping mission. There are two exceptions. First: individual self-defence. Secondly: when the ROE authorize the use of force for the execution of the mission. This is known as mission accomplishment.'[11]

4.1. The Use of Force for Mission Accomplishment

In a letter to the Dutch Parliament, Minister of Defence Kamp writes:

> 'There are three major elements categorizing the legal aspects relating to the dispatching of soldiers:
> a. the mandate or legal basis for the operation;
> b. the rules of engagement and other Instructions on the use of force; and
> c. the status and legal position of the soldiers that are to be dispatched to the area.'[12]

Elements a. and b. defined by the Minister will be discussed on the basis that they can be considered in a 'top-down' approach. The use of force will first be discussed in respect to the mandate, then the ROE, then the Instructions on the use of force. This 'top-down' approach will illustrate how authority travels from the international abstract level to tangible instructions.

The Instructions on the use of force finally serve as the legal basis for the criminal case against Eric O., as described.

---

9 G.L. Coolen, '*Geweldsinstructie*' vanuit strafrechtelijk oogpunt bezien, *Militair Rechtelijk Tijdschrift*, nr. 9, 2003, p. 376.

10 *Ibid.*, p. 385

11 J.A. van Diepenbrugge, Geweldgebruik in het kader van vredesoperaties: leidt de integratie van politieke, juridische en operationele aspecten in de Rules of Engagement in het kader van vredesoperaties tot vage en multi-interpretabele regels?, *Militair Rechtelijk Tijdschrift*, nr. 9, 2003, p. 373.

12 Minister Kamp in a letter to the First Chamber, EK 29200 X, C, April 28, 2004.

4.1.1. The Mandate

As said before, in the 'top-down' approach, the mandate would be the starting point of any analysis of the use of force. In this view, legality would spring from the international rule of law, and then be conveyed down to lower, operational levels. Minister Kamp writes Parliament:

> 'When a mandating resolution for the operation is adopted by the UN Security Council, the planned operation is evaluated to see if it is in accordance with such a mandate and if the size and nature of the dispatchment benefits the objective of the mandate.'[13]

In this view, any dispatchment of troops is therefore in accordance with an international mandate. The mandate dictates legality, when a time of war is non-existent:

> 'In cases other than in time of war, the use of force by soldiers is primarily controlled by the contents of the task attributed.'[14]

Therefore, the mandate is not a statement simply affirming any intervention or peace keeping mission. A mandate will have to address a number of issues; its contents will be broader than an order to take military action on behalf of the international world order. Paphiti:

> 'So, within the context of a UN sponsored operation, the UN Security Council Resolution (the mandate) will set the broad aim of the mission and hopefully address legal issues, such as jurisdiction and powers of stop and search.
> [...]
> It follows that there should be a liaison and discussion, at the highest levels, to ensure that in so far as possible
> a. military requirements are addressed in the mandate, and
> b. tasks flowing from the mandate are fully addressed in the ROE.'[15]

The translation of a mandate into a set of instructions or regulations arguably works both ways as well; the fact that a mandate will address a wide array of legal issues and determine, for example, jurisdiction and legality, also implies that such regulations stemming from a mandate cannot be interpreted with no regard for the mandate they were based on and derived from. Knoops notes:

> 'Therefore the legal qualification of the military Instructions on the use of force cannot be translated into general terms, and such qualification will be greatly dependent upon not just the nature of the military mission but naturally on the (international) mandate for such a military mission as well.'[16]

---

13 *Ibid.*
14 Coolen 2003, *a.w.,* p. 377.
15 Paphiti UK A, *a.w.*, pp. 3-4
16 G.G.J. Knoops, De (inter)nationaal strafrechtelijke betekenis en implicaties van *geweldsinstructies* voor buitenlandse militaire missies, *Delikt en Delinkwent*, nr. 6, 2004, p. 606.

The mandate is a versatile concept; a mandate will embody military, legal and political considerations.

> 'The discussion concerning the mandate, or grounds for the operation, takes place on the tangent plane between law and political desirability and draws the outlines of the international-political crux of international law.'[17]

> 'Therefore, a proper mandate is the result of a symbiosis between law and politics and not just dictation of only one of these two.'[18]

This fusion, as well as the importance of the mandate when interpreting lower level rules and regulations, is illustrated by the Marchal-case.

> Colonel Marchal was the commander of the Belgian detachment dispatched to Rwanda as part of UNAMIR in the early nineties. On April 6th, 1994, the president of Rwanda was killed in an attack. The Prime Minister of Rwanda decided to address the nation on radio. Colonel Marchal was ordered, by the Canadian force-commander Dallaire, to arrange for the armed escort to the radio station. The escort, consisting of Belgian Special Forces, was attacked by Rwandan soldiers and brutally murdered. The Prime Minister was killed as well.
> Colonel Marchal was then charged with death caused by negligent behaviour by the Belgian military court. Though the mandate for UNAMIR dictated that high level Rwandan politicians were to be protected by the UN-forces, Marchal was accused of knowingly putting the Belgian forces at the risk of being attacked by Rwandan military activists seeking the withdrawal of UN-forces from the region.
> The court held that, based on the mandate, the order by commander Dallaire was legitimate and that Marchal was bound to follow the order. He was therefore not to blame for the deaths of the Belgian soldiers.
> This interpretation of the mandate was crucial to the case; only in light of the requirements set by the mandate were Marchal's actions lawful, when they were at the same time punishable by Belgian law.

The Marchal-case is an example of the immediate relevance of the mandate in a criminal case, regardless of the ROE or any additional service regulations. When this view is applied to the case of Eric O., there are certain aspects of the mandate given by the Dutch government that may be relevant to the interpretation of the charges brought against him.

First of all, the status of the Dutch troops in Iraq was fundamentally different from the status of American and British troops. This is mentioned several times in the statements by the government.

Such differences could arguably imply a more restricted policy on the use of force than observed by the British soldiers. Therefore, even though the ROE are adopted from the lead nation – the UK – the difference in status between the lead nation and the Dutch presence in Iraq might imply the wishes of the government to take on more of a peace keeping role in Iraq rather

17 J.F.R. Boddens Hosang, Rules of Engagement: Het politiek-juridische struikelblok voor de militaire commandant, *Militair Rechtelijk Tijdschrift*, nr. 9, 2003, p. 354.

18 *Ibid.*

than an outspoken peace enforcing role. On the other hand, the government clearly states that it believes its ROE to be 'robust' as well as adequate with regard to force protection.

4.1.2. The Rules of Engagement

The Rules of Engagement then translate the mandate to a system of authorizations and prohibitions on an operational level:

> 'Rules of Engagement (ROE) are drafted by the (staff of the) highest ranking military commander of a certain operation. For UN-operations they are drafted by the Department of peacekeeping operations in consultation with the assigned Force Commander, after which they are affirmed by the deputy Secretary-General for peacekeeping operations and made available to the participating nations. The participating nations can then apply additional national restriction in the ROE of their own forces, but no authorization beyond the limitations set, is allowed.'[19]

Major-General Van Diepenbrugge considers the execution of the mandate to be the most relevant factor when drafting the ROE:

> 'The effective execution of the mission should be the leitmotiv for the ROE in my opinion. This mission is described by the mandate in case of peace keeping operations. The assigned and derived tasks, as well as the military means made available implement the mission, whereas the ROE enable adequate action. I have thus defined a triangular relation.'[20]

In the 'top-down' approach, the ROE will serve a more operational function rather than the more political abstractions that may exist in the mandate. Nonetheless, the ROE cannot be considered standing on itself, and exist only within a political context.

> 'The ROE serve a specific military operational goal and provide an instrument to enforce observance of the political aspects.'[21]

4.1.3. The Instructions on the Use of Force

The Instructions on the use of force then further translate the ROE to the level of the individual soldier and his commander. As said before, the Instructions on the use of force have the legal status of a service regulation, whereas the ROE do not have this status according to the initial ruling, but do have this status by the ruling on appeal.

> 'ROE consist of a list of enumerated authorizations or prohibitions of certain uses of force, and, of an Aide-Mémoire (for commanders and senior staff), derived from this list,

19 Minister Kamp in a letter to the First Chamber, EK 29200 X, C, April 28, 2004.
20 Van Diepenbrugge, *a.w.*, p. 372.
21 Minister Kamp in a letter to the First Chamber, EK 29200 X, C, April 28, 2004.

drafted in the national language, and Instructions on the use of force (for the troops). These national charts may include national restrictions on the ROE.'[22]

'Rules of Engagement are aimed primarily at the force-commander. It is his task to translate these guidelines and regulations into instructions the forces under his command are to observe. Usually these instructions are summarized and issued on so-called soldiers cards.'[23]

The authority to use force does not stem from the Instructions on the use of force themselves; the Instructions on the use of force only serve as a translation of the mandate:

'To prevent any misunderstanding, it has to be put first and foremost that the authority (or duty) to use force during a peacekeeping mission does not stem from the applicable Instructions on the use of force, but from the task attributed, from the mandate that is to be implemented.'[24]

The Instructions on the use of force may therefore put further restrictions on the ROE, but may in no way define a broader authorization of the use of force than the ROE drafted by the lead nation.

Based on this relationship, and the position of the Instructions on the use of force in the 'top-down' perspective, it can be argued that only the Instructions on the use of force can authorize the individual soldier to use force. Since the Instructions on the use of force can be of a more restrictive nature than the ROE, any 'by-passing' of the Instructions on the use of force by interpreting this on the basis of the ROE, could potentially undermine this restrictive nature. This would limit the abilities of the government as well as the force-commander to effectively place limitations on any ROE they may consider too permissive. In this view, the legality of the use of force stems from a mandate, whereas the illegality of the use of force arises when the limitations of the Instructions on the use of force are disregarded.

4.2. The Use of Force in Self-defence

Aside from the use of force to accomplish mission objectives, there is also the use of force in self-defence. In a military context, the right to self-defence may require a broader definition than in a civil context, considering that a soldier serves more interests than just his own.

Paphiti writes:

'Within international law, self-defence is a very broad concept and, at the one extreme, recognises the right of an individual to defend himself to, at the other extreme, encompassing the use of military force in pre-emptive self-defence, where there is a genuine perception of an imminent hostile threat (display of hostile intent).

[...]

22 *Ibid.*
23 Coolen 2003, *a.w.*, p. 377.
24 *Ibid.*

The right to act in self-defence, as is often repeated, is an inherent one so it is difficult to see how it can readily be limited by lawful command decision. Indeed, when acting in self-defence, the ROE weapons restrictions are no longer relevant. One is entitled to use all lawful weapon systems available, provided the level of force used is proportionate with the threat or danger posed.'[25]

Paphiti uses the UN-definition of self-defence:

'It is clear that the UN envisages self-defence as including the use of force

a. in the protection of
   - the soldier's own life;
   - the lives of his colleagues;
   - the lives of those entrusted in his care;
   - his post (position defence);
   - his convoy;
   - his vehicle or rifle (military property).
b. where armed persons are attempting to prevent the force from carrying out its mandate, e.g. delivering aid.'[26]

However, Paphiti also argues that self-defence as broadly as it is defined above, can be subject to restrictions:

'However, it is suggested that ROE may properly restrict, in some circumstances, the extent of the application of the right to self-defence. Whereas the defence of oneself, one's unit and friendly forces cannot be lawfully restricted, as these are inherent rights, there is arguably a distinction with the circumstances relating to defence of civilian life, military equipment, and military or civilian property. These considerations are essentially political (although they may be significantly influenced by the views of the military commander) and would be highly relevant in the context of escalation control.'[27]

Boddens Hosang also mentions the possibility of limiting the right to self-defence in the ROE:

'Also, virtually all ROE contain directions for the exercise of the (inherent or not) right to self-defence. In the aforementioned American definition of the ROE, the implementation of the right to self-defence is even defined as one of the objectives of the ROE.'[28]

He does not consider it desirable to impose such limitations:

'Though a statement in the ROE regarding the inviolable right to self-defence could still be considered a general announcement, [...] including rules concerning the right to self-defence in the same ROE would be out of order. If the use of force in self-defence is an

25 Paphiti UK A, *a.w.*, p. 8.
26 *Ibid.*
27 *Ibid.*, p. 9.
28 Boddens Hosang, *a.w.*, p. 360.

inherent right, it follows that this does not have to be confirmed in the form of ROE authorizations'[29]

Boddens Hosang makes a clear distinction between possible use of force in accordance with the ROE, and the use of force in self-defence. This distinction is of consequence to a soldier appealing to his right to self-defence:

> 'Because the right to self-defence can be exercised aside from what is stated in the ROE, the soldier involved needs to be aware of the lack of political or legal warrants when he or she sets aside the carefully drafted framework of the ROE by appealing to his right to self-defence. The right to self- defence is an individual right in this regard as well: one will have to individually justify the decisions made and cannot refer to the ROE or the mission objectives for a given operation. By invoking the emergency measure, one places oneself outside of the structures and warrants of the operational decision making so to speak, and one will have to depend solely on the personal assessment of the situation.'[30]

Knoops notes:

> 'In all the different types of ROE mentioned before, it is emphasized that these do not limit 'the inherent right of self-defence'. The SFOR ROE state that no provision in the SFOR ROE can deny the commander his right and his obligation to take all necessary and adequate measures to exercise the right to self-defence for individual and unit.'[31]

Altogether, one can say that the essence of the right to self-defence authorizes the use of force, regardless of ROE or service regulations. The more broadly the right to self-defence is defined, the more desirable it will be to set limitations in the ROE. Or, when formulated the other way round:

> 'But the nature and content of the military service regulations in force may also determine the range of the meaning of self-defence.'[32]

When applied to the case of Eric O., this means that regardless of the ROE and the Instructions on the use of force, Eric O. would not be punishable if he acted in self-defence. Even if the use of force in self-defence was explicitly prohibited by the ROE, the ROE would be set aside by his right to use force in a situation that calls for self-defence.

The aforementioned Article 41 of the Penal Code recognizes the right to self-defence. In any criminal case the defendant can appeal to this provision. It can be argued that, in any criminal military case, such an appeal should be considered within a military context:

> 'It can therefore be concluded that the term 'self-defence' within the penal context of Article 41 Sr., could be interpreted based on the content of the applicable service regulations

29 *Ibid.*

30 *Ibid.*, p. 361.

31 G.G.J. Knoops, Rules of Engagement – Internationaalrechtelijke, ethische en operationele implicaties, *Marineblad*, December 2002, p. 334.

32 Knoops 2004, *a.w.*, p. 613.

on which the soldier involved based his actions, when he is suspected of committing a criminal act and appealing to his right to self- defence. Aforementioned terms show that the concept of 'force' in a military-operational sense is different in context.'[33]

4.2.1. Situations that call for Self-defence; Hostile Intent, Hostile Act

No fine line can be drawn between situations that allow for self-defence, and situations that do not. It is very hard to come up with a criterion that would definitively make such a distinction. It is better to speak of a spectrum, ranging from situations that allow for any use of force to protect one's own interest, to situations that only allow for a very limited and proportional response to a threat to interests more removed from personal safety.

In military doctrine, there are two concepts that subdivide the part of this spectrum not covered by the classical (civilian) notion of self-defence; the concepts of hostile intent, and hostile act. Knoops:

> 'Most ROE use a special set of concepts, namely hostile intent, and hostile act. These concepts have already been implemented in the definition of self-defence in the jurisprudence of the United States for that matter, contrary to European nations.
> The first concept refers to a hostile intention that has not yet resulted in a concrete attack, whereas hostile act refers to a hostile act that has not yet resulted in a current attack.'[34]

In another publication, he writes:

> 'This is why the MC 362 of the NATO devotes a separate chapter to the interpretation of this difficult set of concepts. It defines, for example, hostile intent as 'not meaning an imminent attack', and hostile act as 'not meaning an actual attack.'[35]

Knoops explicitly relates both concepts to the ROE; in his view, the use of force based on either hostile intent or a hostile act requires a specific basis in the ROE. This contrary to the classical, more limited concept of self-defence, that would authorize immediate use of force, regardless of ROE provisions. He also notes, however, the difficulty of accurately assessing a situation:

> 'To the operational commander, who finds himself confronted with ROE implementing this trident, practical distinctions will quickly become blurred.'[36]

Boddens Hossang also notes the difficulty of any decision to use force in self-defence, regardless of the applicable ROE:

> 'This ultimately leads tot the conclusion that a military commander will often have to make difficult decisions despite the ROE. No degree of clarity or comprehensiveness of

33 *Ibid.*, p. 614.
34 *Ibid.*, p. 613.
35 Knoops 2002, *a.w.*, p. 334.
36 *Ibid.*, p. 335.

the ROE will be able to change that. This goes in particular for decisions regarding the use of force in self-defence, based on a reaction to a hostile act or to hostile intent.'[37]

He then continues to describe the different interpretations of the concepts of hostile act and hostile intent in military doctrine. Referring to two separate publications on doctrine, dating from March 17, 1998 and June 29, 1999, he writes:

> 'There seems to be a striking difference in doctrine regarding the concept of self-defence here, which can be explained by the different publication dates of the handbooks.'[38]

Boddens explains that this difference is due to the fact that the older publication from 1998 still matched the American definition of self-defence. He cites the American definition:

> 'A commander has the authority and obligation to use all necessary means available and to take all appropriate action to defend that commander's unit and other US forces in the vicinity from a hostile act or hostile intent [...].'[39]

Summarized, it is difficult to both categorize a situation as either a hostile act or hostile intent, and define the appropriate response to any such situation. This brings us to the proportionality of the use of force.

4.2.2. Proportionality and Subsidiarity of the Use of Force

When the clear-cut distinction between a situation allowing for self-defence and a situation not allowing for self-defence is relinquished, and the notion of a spectrum, defining self- defence, is assumed, the size and scope of the force used will be subject to limitations of proportionality and subsidiarity. Knoops writes:

> 'The right to self-defence, regardless which part of the spectrum is referred to, is, in other words, inherent, and therefore does not require ROE to be exercised. According to both the *common law* and *civil law* systems, the requirements of proportionality (acting proportional to the threat) and subsidiarity (using the least drastic of means available), will have to be met.'[40]

Jörg writes:

> 'Regardless of the question whether the ROE can be considered an order, Instructions on the use of force do not legitimize every execution imaginable within those Instructions on the use of force. Whatever has been drafted in the Instructions on the use of force for

37 Boddens Hosang, *a.w.*, p. 366.
38 *Ibid.*, p. 367.
39 *Ibid.*
40 Knoops 2004, *a.w.*, p. 613.

> peace keeping: proportionality and subsidiarity will inevitably constitute an unwritten aspect of it.'[41]

When the concept of these requirements is accepted, the distinction between different degrees of self-defence becomes irrelevant; instead, the legality of any exercise of the right to self-defence will now be valued based on the facts of the case and the relationship between the threat and the reaction to the threat.

It can be argued, as is done by Knoops, that the accurate assessment of the situation, as well as the assessment of what would be a proportional and subsidiary response to that situation, should be the subject of a judicial inquiry, rather than the question whether the ROE or service regulations were followed. Knoops mentions the principle of 'a reasonable officer on the scene':

> 'In this regard, perhaps one could choose for the criterion – similar to the interpretation of the Fourth Amendment of the American Constitution by an American judge – that the conduct of a military commander should have been 'objectively reasonable' when force was used, and that such an assessment of his conduct also needs to be based on the circumstances of the case the soldier involved was confronted with.'[42]

5. The Initial Ruling

There are some aspects of the trial that concern legal questions relating to what has been discussed above. As said before, Eric O. was charged with the violation of a service regulation, the Instructions on the use of force. The relation between the ROE and the Instructions on the use of force plays a key role in the Court's decision.

Also, the Court decides on a burden of proof based on the defendant's status of soldier.

5.1 The Legal Status of the ROE and the Instructions on the Use of Force

> 'The rules stated in the ROE were in force during the period the indictment refers to. The SFIR Instructions on the use of force and the Aide-Mémoire for SFIR commanders are service regulations consisting of a summary of the most important rules and obligations set by the ROE, translated to the level of the commander on the scene (Aide-Mémoire) and the soldier/marine (Instructions on the use of force).
> [...]
> The Court notes that the AM refers to the ROE for further explanation. The Aide-Mémoire/Instructions on the use of force serve to improve legal security and to provide warrants for the individual soldier executing his tasks under operational circumstances. Therefore, the Aide-Mémoire and Instructions on the use of force need to make absolutely clear what is and what is not authorized.'[43]

---

41 N. Jörg, Een opmerking over de reikwijdte van het beroep op ambtelijk bevel en een opmerking over de delictskeuze van de officier van justitie, in militaribus, *Militair Rechtelijk Tijdschrift*, nr. 9, 2003, p. 391.

42 Knoops 2004, *a.w.*, pp. 620-621.

43 Rechtbank Arnhem, 18 Oktober 2004, LJN AR4029.

As said before, the Court finds that the Aide-Mémoire and the Instructions on the use of force are both service regulations as defined by Article 135 WMSr, whereas the ROE are of a different nature (see I.D).

5.2. The Burden of Proof

In its decision, the Court rules that only a reasonable explanation is required when the necessity of the use of force is assessed. A soldier does not have to prove beyond any doubt that his actions were called for:

> 'When assessing the necessity of the use of force, the Military Chamber considers, in accordance with previous rulings by court martials, that, regarding the necessity of the use of force, a soldier cannot be demanded to prove more than the fact that a reasonable explanation for his behaviour existed, and that the incorrectness of such an explanation can only be established when the falsity of his explanation is made plausible.'[44]

The public prosecution service will later appeal this part of the ruling, stating that a burden of proof, only requiring a soldier to reasonably explain his behaviour, would not be in accordance with developments in military law.

The ruling 'favours' a defendant charged with illegal use of force, leaving it up to the pubic prosecution service to prove the use of force was not necessary, rather than placing the burden of proof of the necessity of such use of force on the defendant.

5.3. The Situation

With regard to the situation, the Court finds that a threat existed, and that this threat could have escalated into an unstable situation:

> 'Based on the foregoing, defendant could reasonably consider the situation a threat and the situation could develop in a way that would directly endanger the safety of the unit, within a short period of time.
>
> [...]
>
> Defendant remained confronted with a situation that posed a potential risk to safety as well as defendant's freedom of action, a situation calling for action.'

Based on military doctrine discussed above, it can therefore be argued that the situation could be qualified as either *hostile intent*, or a *hostile act*. Though no imminent danger existed, the potential of such danger was present. It is also clear that the situation did not fall under a classical, narrower definition of self-defence; no immediate danger existed, no attack was carried out on the defendant or his unit.

44 *Ibid.*

5.4. The Instructions on the Use of Force did not Authorize a Warning Shot under Circumstances

The Court finds:

> 'Considering the previously described threat, and also considering defendant's statement during the trial ('the situation was not as threatening as to fire an aimed shot'), the Military Chamber finds that the imminent danger was not immediately present. No situation stated in points 3 and 4 of the Aide-Mémoire and in point 2 of the Instructions on the use of force existed, allowing for the use of deadly force consisting of firing an aimed shot, now that no immediate threat was present.
> [...]
> Rules regarding the firing of warning shots are drafted in the Instructions on the use of force (point 12 in relation to point 11) and in the Aide-Mémoire (point 8 in relation with points 6 and 7). Aforementioned points link the firing of a warning shot to a situation that allows for the use of deadly force.'

No legality of the firing of a warning shot could be based on the Instructions on the use of force under the circumstances present during the incident; since the Instructions on the use of force only allow for the use of warning shots when the situation authorizes the use of deadly force. It is important to note how the Instructions on the use of force explicitly authorize the firing of warning shots in situations allowing for the use of deadly force (as defined in point 2 of the Instructions on the use of force). It may therefore be argued that the Instructions on the use of force also intend to *limit* the authorization to fire warning shots to such situations calling for deadly force.

5.5. The ROE did Authorize Warning Shots under Circumstances

Despite the Instructions on the use of force, however, the Court finds that warning shots were authorized by the ROE:

> 'Since a situation allowing for the use of deadly force did not exist, the question needs to be answered whether the warning shot could be legitimate on other grounds. To do so the ROE can be consulted, considering that the opening remarks of the Aide-Mémoire state that the ROE apply.
> Under number 151, the ROE state (summarized), that warnings can be given through any means if warnings are necessary for the execution of the mission. This implies that the use of a warning shot as an independent means of force (other than a warning shot as a preface to deadly force) can be authorized.
> The Military Chamber finds that the warning shots fired by suspect can be and should be based on the rule of ROE nr. 151, [...].'

5.6. Acquittal

Considering that the ROE authorized the firing of warning shots, and the fact that Eric O.'s response was proportionate and subsidiary, the Court acquits Eric O.

6. Appeal

On October 29, 2004, the public prosecution service decides to appeal the decision by the Court.

> 'The public prosecution service in Arnhem does not agree with the verdict by the Military Chamber of the Arnhem District Court. The position adopted by the court does not create enough space for an objective review of the conduct of soldiers and therefore complicates a criminal investigation into the use of force.
> [...]
> During the shooting incident, an innocent civilian died. He was not a plunderer. The public prosecution service has taken into consideration Eric O.'s position (such as the fact that he will have to face the situation for a longer time period), the extensive public interest and the discussion on the tasks and position of the public prosecution service. The administration of justice in two instances is of great importance to the Dutch legal system. The need for objective review of the use of force in question and the legal issue involved justify the use of existing legal options.
> [...]
>
> **Legal and factual grounds**
> [...]
> - The presumption of facts by the court does not create enough space for an objective review of the conduct of the persons involved. The court, when assuming the likeliness of Eric O.'s statements, wholly disregards the technical evidence and a number of witness statements.
> - The court has overextended the range of the service regulations.
> [...]
> The court then introduces the concept of a 'potential threat' that allows the firing of warning shots, according to the court. The public prosecution service disagrees with this view.
> - In the opinion of the public prosecution service, the court has incorrectly found that Eric O.'s actions were proportionate and subsidiary while firing the warning shot, for the verdict does not indicate that the court has weighed in the (considerable) risk of a ricochet of a warning shot in the ground. According to expert witnesses during the trial, there is the risk of a ricochet when firing into the ground, causing (parts of) the bullet to behave unpredictably, having enough residual energy to lethally hit someone.'[45]

45 Press report Distsrict Court Arnhem, October 29, 2004.

7. The Ruling on Appeal by the Military Chamber of the Arnhem Court of Appeal

7.1. The Legal Status of the ROE and the Instructions on the Use of Force

As mentioned before, the ruling on appeal is very different from the initial ruling with regard to the legal qualification of the ROE and the Instructions on the use of force. According to the Court, the ROE do qualify as a service regulation under Dutch law.

> 'b5. The Court finds that the ROE meet the demands set by Article 135 of the Military Penal Code for a service regulation.
> [...]
> They constitute a written decision of a general nature, clearly relate to a soldier's duties and contain authorizations and limitations addressed at the soldier. This is not changed by the fact that the ROE first and foremost describe authorizations, considering that a breach of authorization is always illegal.
> The objection by the counsel's statements, that the ROE are not service regulations considering their secret nature, is rejected by the court. As considered before, the ROE are well known by dispatched soldiers.
> [...]
> For the sake of completeness, the court notes that the fact that the ROE are drafted in English, does not change the court's opinion with regard to the nature of the service regulation. The international dimension of these kinds of dispatchments requires the predominant use of the English language.'

On the relation between the ROE and the Instructions on the use of force, the Court finds:

> 'e1. Both the Aide-Mémoire and the Instructions on the use of force are, as explicitly stated by expert witness [involved 3] during the trial, simplified derivatives of the mother-document, the ROE. If the Aide-Mémoire or the Instructions on the use of force say 'authorized', this is not meant limitative. Further authorizations are just not listed on the cards. The most extensive authorizations are listed in the mother-document.
> The Court finds that the CDS has made this very clear, noting the quoted beginning of the Aide-Mémoire. Despite the lack of a similar reference in the Instructions on the use of force, the Court finds that the same goes for the Instructions on the use of force.'

This leads to an important conclusion:

> 'e2. Noting the aforementioned, the Court finds that the use of force not covered by the Aide-Mémoire or the Instructions on the use of force do not constitute a violation of a service regulation, when operating within the margins of the ROE.'

Though it might seem that this conclusion is similar to the initial ruling, the difference is noteworthy; the Court does not attach any value to the Instructions on the use of force, when it would contradict or limit the ROE. Now that the ROE qualify as a service regulation under

Dutch law (despite its clear international nature), the Instructions on the use of force seem to become almost irrelevant.

7.2. The Situation

On the situation leading to the warning shots, the Court finds:

> 'd. As the Court has mentioned before, defendant, being commander, had to assess the situation as a whole, which of course implies he has some discretion. The Court finds that suspect remained within the limitations of the authorization given by ROE 151, noting 'commanders intent' with regard to 'force property' and the requirements of 'force protection' when a breach of security is imminent.
>
> e. Defendant was allowed to fire warning shots, based on the aforementioned. Noting the circumstances at the time, particularly the fact that shots in the air had not had the desirable effect, it cannot be said that a shot in the ground in a spot deemed safe, should be deemed grossly negligent, or considerably negligent, careless, or neglectful.'

7.3. Acquittal

Eric O. is then acquitted by the Court.

7.4. Additional Considerations

In the reactions on the ruling on appeal, the general consensus was that the court had been unusual critical about the role of the public prosecution service in the case. De Wijkerslooth was even mentioned by name in the ruling, a very uncommon statement.

The Court, for example, concludes:

> '[...] The court acknowledges that the willingness to cooperate has to come from both sides ('it takes two to tango'), but has to conclude to its regret, that in this case, the public prosecution service was apparently unprepared with regard to the question, how to handle a shooting incident like this. This has lead to, especially in the beginning, a far too grave assessment of the case, as mentioned before when the admissibility of the case was discussed.
>
> [...]
>
> In cases such as the one at hand, the result can be that the public prosecution service would deny a soldier the necessary legal backing during his work under difficult circumstances. The public prosecution service will have to develop the required 'situation awareness', just like the soldier sent on a mission to foreign conflict areas.'

With regard to the '*praesumptio innocentiae*', the court refers to Mr De Wijkerslooth;[46] Eric O.'s counsel had argued that a fair trial was made impossible by the actions of the public prosecution service:

46 Mr De Wijkerslooth was head of the public prosecution service during the time of Eric O.'s case.

> 'The court finds that the public prosecution service has initially assessed the case far too grave. The public prosecution service, in particular Mr De Wijkersolooth during his NOVA-interview on January 5, 2004, has also not observed the preferred reservedness during the early stage of the investigation.'

Commenting on the investigation itself, the Court finds:

> 'The court finds that the investigation has indeed been incomplete. The failure to hear the Dutch battalion commander, lieutenant-colonel [involved 1], the failure to submit the relevant 'situational reports' (sitreps) and the incomplete forensic investigation are ever so many hiatus. The court does not find, however, that such mistakes have been made, that, in all reason, prosecution should not have taken place on the ground of the dossier before us.'

A somewhat awkward consideration is found at the end of the verdict:

> 'e. The Court has concluded, during the investigation in this case, that experienced soldiers do not in general consider firing in the ground with a subsoil as was present at the location, more dangerous than a shot in the air. Based on the second investigation with shooting tests by the expert [involved 6], doubt could arise about the validity of such a notion. 50% of the shots fired turned out to ricochet, with an almost unpredictable, dangerous effect within a considerably large area behind the target. A further, especially more extensive, investigation into the phenomenon of ricochet seems called for, as well as – if required – an adjustment of the shooting training and shooting instructions.'

Part III – Political Aspects

1. Introduction

The case of Eric O. has had considerable political ramifications. The case also caused public disapproval of the way it was handled. These sentiments were directed primarily at the responsible authorities, particularly the public prosecution service. The performance by procureur-generaal De Wijkerslooth, head of the public prosecution service, only made matters worse, to an extent that the Minister of Justice who is politically responsible for the public prosecution service, had to rush to Parliament to explain what was going on.

On two areas, the influence of the incident has been most significant: first, the relation between the public prosecution service and the political system (in particularly when relating to the prosecution of members of the armed forces). Secondly, the case will have serious consequences for the deployment of troops abroad and the legal aspects pertaining to such a deployment. It can easily be imagined that the Dutch government would want this case to remain unique in its kind. This third part of the essay will briefly review some reactions, political and other, to the incident.

2. Reactions to the Incident

Minister Kamp, in his 2004 New Year's speech:

> 'The government did not send social workers to Iraq, nor civilian police, but soldiers. They are part of the Quick Reaction Force that acts when necessary. Action needs to be taken against plundering. It starts with one truck, five the next time, and eventually a whole transport. Before you know, it's trouble. This needs to be prevented.'[1]

State Secretary Van der Knaap, while addressing the detachment for SFIR II that had returned to the Netherlands, March 18, 2004:

> 'Nonetheless I cannot ignore the shooting incident that took place right after Christmas. It must have strongly affected you. Here too, five thousand kilometres away, it has had a lot of impact. Everybody had an opinion on it. Politicians, experts, the proverbial know-it-alls, reporters, you name it.
> It is remarkable that most of the people in the discussion had never heard of Instructions on the use of force, let alone know its contents. You have dealt with this in an admirably professional manner. You have kept your heads cool and your backs straight. Based on that Instructions on the use of force – you did know what it stated – you have continued your work. As professionals. This is greatly to your credit. It was only the next day, when shots were fired again. Shortly after, you have arrested criminal elements. You did not sit down under it. On the contrary. You have done your job and let the discussion be the dis-

1 Minister Kamp, speech of January 15, 2004.

cussion. By doing so you have indicated your faith in our judicial system. For this professional attitude, I have enormous respect.'[2]

Mr De Wijkerslooth, in his letter, dated the same day:

'The Iraq-issue
Displeasure predominated the public judgement of the position the Arnhem Office of the Public Prosecutor took in the Iraq-matter.
[...]

The suspicion
Based on the first results of the investigation and the desire to take the soldier involved into custody, the suspicion became murder, manslaughter, or involuntary manslaughter.
The suspicion of murder was based on the deliberate shot and the statement by a military witness who stated that he saw the suspect aim his weapon at the crowd, then look through his visor and subsequently fire. With regard to the variation of manslaughter, it can be said that in case of a ricochet, suspect apparently accepted the risk of a lethal hit when firing into the ground.

The Instructions on the use of force
The Netherlands is not an occupying power in Iraq. The SFIR mission is to contribute to the creation of a safe and stable environment to enable the reconstruction of the country as well as a transition to representative self-government.
Consequently, the Instructions on the use of force contain additional restrictions to the Rules of Engagement. Suspect claims that he fired two warning shots. The Instructions on the use of force do not define a warning shot. Nonetheless, a warning shot is generally considered use of force, which was not allowed according to the Instructions on the use of force.
In this case, a very grave suspicion exists that the victim was hit by a bullet fired by the suspect. He therefore has not fired in a safe direction. Suspect is a very experienced sharpshooter. He should have taken into account the possibility of a ricochet.
[...]

Publicity
Displeasure also existed regarding the publicity policy pursued. Why did the public prosecution service actively announce this case? And why did Mr De Wijkerslooth go on Nova? The answer to the first question is short: The public prosecution service did not announce the case. It was agreed upon with the Arnhem Office of the Public Prosecutor not to give publicity to this case. On January 2nd however it confirmed to a Parliamentary journalist of the Algemeen Nederlands Persbureau (ANP) that it was investigating into a possible suspicion.
[...]
While on Nova, I particularly commented on the manner in which the public prosecution service handles the case, and on the investigation.'[3]

---

2 State secretary Van der Knaap, speech of March 18, 2004.
3 Letter by Mr J.M. De Wijkerslooth, President of the Council of Public Prosecutors, to the Heads of the District Courts and others, confidential letter of January 15, 2004.

This television show appearance becomes more understandable when taken into consideration the reaction to the prosecution of Eric O. Van der Burg writes:

> 'The public prosecution service's decision in the Eric O.-case led to astonishment and alarm in the Netherlands, and to bitterness and insecurity among marines in Iraq.'[4]

This appearance of the highest ranking official within the public prosecution service on television causes political uproar. Member of Parliament Bakker (D66[5]) asks the Ministers of Justice and Defence:

> '2. Who announced the incident on late December 28th? How do you explain the fact that announcements were initially neutral, whereas only a few days later a person involved was arrested and charged with murder, manslaughter, or death through negligence?
>
> 3. Understanding the fact that certain issues can not be addressed pending an investigation, can you nonetheless indicate why the public prosecution service already disclosed the charge (murder, manslaughter or death through negligence), when the investigation has not yet been completed according to Mr de Wijkerslooth? Did the public prosecution service start the judicial investigation itself, or were charges pressed? If the latter is the case, who pressed charges?
>
> 4. Do you agree with Mr De Wijkerslooth, that action taken in Iraq under these circumstances, can be compared to action by the police in the Netherlands? In such cases of police actions in the Netherlands, how is the officer involved dealt with? Would he be arrested immediately, or do different procedures apply?
> [...]
>
> 6. Do you feel the Instructions on the use of force are clear? Did any uncertainty about the interpretation of the Instructions on the use of force in similar cases arise among soldiers? Is it true that shooting incidents took place after December 27th? Were there injuries? Will such incidents be investigated by the public prosecution service? Have there been shooting incidents prior to December 27th? How were they dealt with?'[6]

Minister Kamp, also on behalf of the Minister of Justice, answers:

> '2 and 3. The incident was announced by the information board of the Ministry of Defence on December 28th. The announcement indicated that the incident had occurred and that the Military Police had started an investigation.
> In response to questions from the ANP, the spokesman for the court of Arnhem specified the request to take suspect into custody. The qualifications used by the spokesman related to the suspicion that had arisen against the arrested soldier.

---

4 F.H. van der Burg, Militair strafrecht zonder nucleaire paraplu, *Nederlands Juristenblad*, September 17, 2004, nr. 33, p. 1737.

5 Democraten '66, Dutch political party.

6 *Aanhangsel*, session year 2003-2004, 761.

When the investigation is closed, the public prosecution service decides whether it will prosecute the suspected soldier. Only if the public prosecution service decides to subpoena the suspect in front of a judge, the final indictment will be formulated.
[...]
4. Military actions in Iraq and civilian actions to maintain public safety are similar in that an investigation will follow in both situations if the use of a firearm has resulted in death or injury. When suspicion arises that a police officer has committed a crime, he will be marked suspect.

6. The violence instructions are clear. [...] No shooting incidents occurred that led to further investigation.'[7]

Prime Minister Balkenende visits the Dutch troops stationed in As Samawah after the incident. With regard to this incident, Member of Parliament Vos (GroenLinks[8]) asks the Prime Minister:

'1. Is it true that, during your visit of the troops stationed at As Samawah, you have expressed your opinion on the investigation and prosecution actions taken by public prosecution service officials in the matter of the shooting incident on December 27th, 2003? If so, is it true that you have said that the arrest of the soldier involved was 'not a decision by Defence or politics'? Do you mean to say that, as a member of the government, you do not wish to take responsibility for decisions made by the public prosecution service?'[9]

Prime Minister Balkenende answers:

'1 and 2. The Prime Minister has wanted to express that the public prosecution service, as usual, independently decided to start an investigation. As a rule, members of the government are not involved in individual criminal cases. This approach is partly based on the desire to prevent any (party)political influence in such matters. Besides, reservedness befits the legislative and executive branch when a case is still under investigation and a judge (presumably) still has to rule on the case.'[10]

Members of Parliament Balemans and Griffith (VVD[11]), in addition to Mr Bakker, also demand an explanation for Mr De Wijkerslooth's appearance on Nova:

'1. Were you aware of Mr De Wijkerslooth's statements regarding the shooting incident in Iraq involving a Dutch marine prior to the airing?
[...]
3. To what extent do the procedures of the public prosecution service, de 'Koninlijke Marechaussee' and the police for dealing with shooting incidents involving soldiers or police-officers, differ?
4. What is your opinion on Mr De Wijkerslooths' performance?
5. What measures do you intend to take to prevent such performances in the future?'[12]

7 *Ibid.*
8 Dutch political party.
9 *Aanhangsel*, session year 2003-2004, 724.
10 *Ibid.*
11 Volkspartij voor Vrijheid en Democratie, Dutch political party.

The Minister of Justice, Donner, replies:

> '1. Prior to the broadcast, I was informed of the intended participation of Mr De Wijkerslooth in the TV-program Nova on January 5th, 2004.
> 2, 4 and 5. This is a criminal case with exceptional aspects. Though the facts of the case are still the subject of an investigation and great caution needs to be exercised when making remarks about it, the great social interest has prompted Mr De Wijkersloonth to appear on Nova.
> [...]
> I do not consider Mr De Wijkersllooth's appearance irresponsible. I therefore do not see the necessity to take measures.
> 3. Now that the actions by the Dutch soldiers involved a conflict with the local population, a comparison can be made in this respect with the maintaining of public order by riot police.
> There are of course important differences like, for example, the conditions under which the soldiers operate, the legal framework applying to their actions, the training of the persons involved and the fact that a soldier is not a criminal investigator.
> When a police-officer kills a civilian while maintaining public order, a thorough investigation will be conducted. When suspicion of a crime arises in this regard, there are no procedural differences. It is true however that the Council of Public Prosecutors has passed the instruction on the position of a police official regarding the use of force (*instructie positie politiefunctionaris bij geweldsaanwending*) of 16-05-2000, relating to the investigation into cases of the use of force by a police officer while in function. This instruction of course does not apply to soldiers.'[13]

To comment on his appearance on national television, as well as to comment on another unrelated matter, De Wijkersllooth writes a letter to all heads of the public prosecution service divisions. Unfortunately, a month after he writes the letter it somehow leaks to the press. The passage relating to the Instructions on the use of force becomes controversial within days. To some it suggests that Dutch troops in Iraq have to fight with their hands tied behind their backs.

When the letter leaks, the Ministers of Defence and Justice are forced to respond. They do so in writing to Parliament:

> 'Reports in the media that the public prosecution service holds the view that Dutch soldiers part of the multinational stabilization force in Iraq are not allowed to use force, are incorrect.
> [...]
> The passage in this letter relating to the Instructions on the use of force, has been interpreted incorrectly. It has been wrongly suggested that the public prosecution service holds the view that soldiers in Iraq are not allowed to use force in general, including the firing of warning shots. This is incorrect. There is no difference in opinion regarding the Instructions on the use of force. As said, the passage mentioned relates to a specific case.
> Differences between the Dutch Instructions on the use of force and the 'Rules of Engagement' of the United Kingdom as an occupying power, do not relate to the use of

12 *Aanhangsel*, session year 2003-2004, 774.
13 *Ibid.*

force when guarding or securing properties, nor do they relate to the circumstances during the incident on December 27th, 2003. In this regard, no restrictions apply to Dutch units as a result of not being a part of the occupying powers.
[...]
During a recent visit to Iraq by the ministers of Defence and Foreign Affairs, it was once again confirmed that no confusion exists among the Dutch soldiers in Iraq with regard to the Instructions on the use of force and their application.'[14]

In a meeting between the Parliamentary committees on Defence, Justice and Foreign Affairs, and the Ministers on March 18, 2004, the issue is thoroughly discussed, in particular the passage about the Instructions on the use of force. Koenders (PvdA[15]):

'Contrary to the government, the public prosecution service finds that Dutch soldiers are more limited in the use of force than British soldiers being an occupying power. The letter by the government masks these differences and puts the public prosecution service in a corner. The public prosecution service has acted in a clumsy and obstinate way, for which the Minister of Justice is (politically) responsible.'[16]

Minister of Defence Kamp:

'For example, soldiers will always have to take into consideration the principles of proportionality and subsidiarity. Any use of force has to be careful. Soldiers must first hesitate and think, and only then do what is necessary.
[...]
There is no gap between the Rules of Engagement and the Instructions on the use of force. Rules of engagement have a non-specific nature. Instructions on the use of force are an implementation of the ROE.'[17]

Wilders (then VVD, independent now):

'It is important that the Ministers of Defence and Justice have made clear that soldiers will not be prosecuted when they observe the Instructions on the use of force, which are robust and thorough.
[...]
Letters should always be well written and never be multi-interpretable. It would have graced the minister if he had just said that it was clumsy and that he will correct it. Politicians sometimes have to bite the dust a little.'[18]

14 Letter by Mr J.M. De Wijkerslooth, President of the Council of Public Prosecutors, to the Heads of the District Courts and others, confidential letter of January 15, 2004.
15 Partij van de Arbeid, Dutch political party.
16 TK 23432, nr. 152, March 18, 2004.
17 *Ibid.*
18 *Ibid.*

3. The Public Prosecution Service

As said before, the role of the public prosecution service in the case of Eric O. is controversial. Van der Burg discusses the role of the public prosecution service in military cases in general in an article on criminal military law. On the public prosecution service, he writes:

> 'The fact that the public prosecution service has sought more publicity than normal in the Eric O.-case, had led to the belief that the interpretation of the Instructions on the use of force is primarily a task of the public prosecution service. This is incorrect. The Instructions on the use of force are issued by the Minister of Defence and the regulation should be interpreted by Defence as well. The commander of the dispatched unit is in charge of having the soldiers involved observe the Instructions on the use of force. The public prosecution service can and must judge in retrospect whether a soldier who used force is punishable, but the public prosecution service cannot judge in advance and in general the illegality of certain uses of force.'[19]

Parliament demands changes in the legal system to prevent any occurrences of similar cases in the future. Minister Donner mentions the questions raised about the competence of the public prosecution service in military cases:

> 'During the consultation with the permanent Parliamentary committee on Defence on February 27th last, (*Kamerstuk*[20] 23432, nr. 152) I have promised to inform Parliament together with the permanent committee on Justice in writing, about the military expertise of the public prosecution service.
> [...]
> During aforementioned consultation, concern was expressed with the way the public prosecution service acts in cases involving a criminal investigation into soldiers. It has been suggested that the Arnhem Office of the Public Prosecutor, being responsible for the investigation and prosecution of crimes involving soldiers in first instance, does not have the disposal of sufficient and relevant military expertise to act in a manner inspiring trust in complex and sensitive matters.'[21]

He then lists a number of measures taken to ensure the questioned expertise, such as training and practical experience, frequent consultations of liaison officers and military experts, and finally the review of all activities of the public prosecution service relating to investigation and prosecution by the trial judges, one of which is a member of the armed forces in accordance with Article 5 of the Military Penal Code of Procedure.

---

19 Van der Burg, *a.w.*, p. 1738.
20 Parliamentary document.
21 TK 29200 VI, No. 130, March 30, 2004.

3.1. The Relationship between the Department of Defence and the Public Prosecution Service

On July 9, 2004, Minister Kamp lists a number of agreements reached between the two departments as well, as he promised Parliament to do:

> 'The instruction chart for the use of force, in Dutch, will be made available to the public prosecution service, prior to the first detachment part of a new operation, as well as every subsequent change made. The same goes for operations involving a Dutch 'Aide-Mémoire for Commanders'.
> [...]
> There will be more frequent consultations between the public prosecution service and Defence, also on operational or (operational-)legal questions that could not already be answered by the liaison officer.
> [...]
> Prior to dispatchments of troops of considerable size, the public prosecution service will receive a briefing by the Ministry of Defence. The briefing will address, among other things, the regulations for the use of force, status agreements (including agreements on jurisdiction) and the mandate for the operation.'[22]

On these agreements, Van der Burg writes:

> 'Minister Kamp has now informed Parliament of several forms of consultation between Defence and the public prosecution service in a letter of July 9th (*Kamerstukken II* 03-04, 29521, nr. 6.) These are a number of measures to merely improve relations, rather than concrete procedures on decision-making.'[23]

4. The Military Judicial System

The uniqueness of the Dutch military judicial system is emphasized by Van der Burg. In his contribution, he puts this system in a historical perspective and questions whether it functions properly under modern circumstances.

> 'The integration of military law within regular jurisdiction is unique. As far as I have been able to verify, a somewhat similar system exists only in France, but in France different systems apply to crimes committed within or outside of Republic territory.
> [...]
> When the government decided to participate in a multinational stabilization force in Iraq with a marine battalion, it was assumed, without due consideration, that the integrated system of military jurisdiction would function properly with regard to Dutch soldiers in Iraq.
> [...]
> The Dutch armed forces did train for a war in Central Europe, but actually led a calm existence under the umbrella of nuclear deterrence. The new penal and disciplinary code

22 TK 29521, No. 6, July 9, 2004.
23 Van der Burg, *a.w.*, p. 1739.

> adapted perfectly to these years of life in the barracks. It is the irony of history that the new military penal and disciplinary codes were drafted the year the Cold War ended with the German reunification. This reunification meant the beginning of the deformation of the Warsaw-pact. The threat of an attack by the Soviet Union and its satellite states was replaced with the threat of smaller conflicts between parties immune to nuclear deterrence, not even mentioning suicide attacks that are not influenced by any deterrence at all. The armed forces need to commit to participation in conflicts taking place in countries far away and not involving the defence of the homeland. It will really be a time of war over there, but it will be peace time in the Arnhem district, and the Office of the Public Prosecutor of this peaceful district will have to judge the way Dutch soldiers carry the sorrows of the world.'[24]

It seems to be the '*opinio communis*' that the public prosecution service does not have the experience or manpower to adequately deal with military cases. In this somewhat narrow view, the system is primarily judged upon the acts of the prosecution; whether such a view is an accurate one, does not fall within the area of discussion covered by this paper.

5. The Trial of Eric O.

Nonetheless, the trial of Eric O. has had its questionable moments. Van der Burg notes the apprehension on murder charges:

> 'The Council of Public Prosecutors stated, in a confidential (but leaked) letter of January 15th, 2004: "Based on the first results of the investigation and the desire to take the soldier involved into custody, the suspicion became murder, manslaughter, or involuntary manslaughter." I consider this an incorrect approach. A provisional suspicion can be a ground for custody, but the desire to take someone into custody cannot determine the suspicion murder or manslaughter. Moreover, there was little opportunity in the Netherlands for a proper investigation, by hearing Iraqi witnesses for example.'[25]

It does seem strange that the eventual charge against Eric O. is only a violation of service regulations; this in particular has led some to believe that the public prosecution service dealt with the Eric O. trial as a matter of prestige rather than judge the case on its legal merits.

6. The Instructions on the Use of Force/ROE

The Eric O. case almost became synonymous with the legal use of force. Members of Parliament rushed to the microphone to ensure that proper force could legally be used by Dutch soldiers. It seems that this might be the most important contribution of the trial to public debate: the use of force as an inherent right of any soldier. Member of Parliament Bakker (D66) asks the Minister of Defence:

---

24 *Ibid.*, pp. 1736, 1739.
25 *Ibid.*, p. 1736.

'1. Is it true that the Instructions on the use of force for Dutch soldiers was adjusted due to the transition of sovereignty on June 28th late?
2. If so, in what way and with what significance? What adjustments have been made to the original Instructions on the use of force?'[26]

The Minister answers:

'1. Yes
2. and 3. A letter to Parliament of June 11th, stated that the transition of sovereignty could have implications for the Instructions on the use of force. The Instructions on the use of force cannot be disclosed in order not to endanger the safety of Dutch troops. This is also true with the instruction card for the use of force. Nonetheless it can be said in general that the instructions regarding self-defence have not become more restrictive.'[27]

The more complex dimensions of the use of force were already discussed by scholars. In his article on the complexity of ROE, Boddens Hosang notes, for example:

'The model proposed by Roach in 1983 for the ROE is basically still usable for drafting and analysing ROE. Some changes that have occurred since then require however a more differentiated approach to the model. This goes particularly for the increased attention to the individual penalization and prosecution based on actions taken during military operations, the increasing media coverage of the deployment of troops and the increased political risks relating to military operations. This last-mentioned factor partly relates to the increased media attention, and for the rest relates to the increase in political decisions involving the deployment of military means on grounds other than the classical legal ones.'[28]

It seems that clarity will be vital in future legal discussions on drafting ROE and Instructions on the use of force when these reactions are taken into consideration. No ambiguity will be tolerated by the responsible politicians, even when this requires that more complex situations as mentioned in the second part of the essay (remember hostile intent and hostile act), are not or too easily dealt with.

7. The Second Leak

To end this 'slide show' of political and social uproar as a result of the incident, it would serve to quote some reactions to the second leak in the Eric O.-case, when an attachment to the initial letter of De Wijkerslooth was also leaked to the press; this attachment revealed that Eric O. had been involved in secret and special operations in the past, and he was described as '*laagdrempelig*' when it comes to the use of force, a word that, in the context, might best be translated as (to some extent) 'trigger-happy'.

---

26 *Aanhangsel*, session year 2003-2004, nr. 2269.
27 *Ibid.*
28 Boddens Hosang, *a.w.*, p. 366.

Koenders (PvdA):

> 'Mr Chairman. For the third time this year, the Second Chamber needs to address a matter that should just be dealt with by the public prosuction service, and doing so should result in a speedy decision about a possible prosecution of Eric O.
> My fraction finds this serious and dangerous. We will again not discuss the merits of the case tonight. That is not up to us. Fortunately, this country does not know political justice. This makes it even worse that, after the cursed performance by Mr De Wijkerslooth on Nova and the infamous letter to the Offices of the Public Prosecutor that caused general confusion, particularly among the men and women in Iraq, about the Instructions on the use of force, Eric O.'s dossier regarding highly sensitive and dangerous missions by the special assistance unit, is out on the streets.
> [...]
> How much longer can this puppet-show in the Eric O.-case continue, now that it keeps resulting in ever more safety and political risks?'[29]

Herben (LPF[30]):

> 'It is unacceptable to the LPF-party, that the names of soldiers risking their lives in service of our country, are leaked. The prosecution policy of the public prosuction service is an open nerve with the LPF fraction. I do not deny that. Salt has now been rubbed into this wound in an unacceptable manner. We have a public prosuction service in this country, showing misplaced initiative. Storekeepers who defend themselves are prosecuted, but criminals get away with anything. This is a matter of failing leadership. One fails to set the right priorities. The limited capacity of police and justice should be used in ways that best serve the rule of law. The LPF-party feels it is time that Minister Donner calls De Wijkerslooth to order. In this country, the public prosuction service is not an autonomous organ answering to no one. Mr De Wijkerslooth is a high level official who answers to the Minister of Justice. He has to do little more than what he is instructed to do by the Minister of Justice. It is therefore time for the Minister of Justice to intervene in this matter.'[31]

29 TK 29200-X, nr. 85, June 16, 2004.
30 Lijst Pim Fortuyn, Dutch political party.
31 *Ibid.*

Conclusion

The Eric O.-case, and perhaps any criminal case, is far too complex to be properly discussed in a 50-page essay. This is particularly true when one has limited or no access to the case files. Nonetheless, a considerable part of the ramifications of the case do not necessarily relate to criminal law.

The Arendt-dilemma described in the introduction of the essay, perfectly grasps the difficulty of warfare in the 21st century; in the view of the authors, the Eric O.-case is an example of this complexity. On the one hand, members of the armed forces need to be able to successfully accomplish the missions given to them; on the other hand, the use of force may to some extent be a Pandora's Box: once invoked, it can in no way be undone, and can be compensated for only to a limited degree.

The judicial and political 'chaos' following the incident has only complicated this situation. To the public at large, the image now exists that Dutch soldiers are sent abroad with 'water pistols'. To the soldiers involved, no degree of clarity offered by the ROE or Instructions on the use of force might change their fundamental concepts on the use of force and the impact of the Eric O. case on their views. It has become very clear to them that even the highest authorities in the country do not know how to deal with deadly force, regardless of its legality.

It needs to be mentioned that the innocence of Eric O. seems to be beyond any doubt in the opinion of many. The fact that a civilian causality was caused by Eric O.'s actions has in no way affected this view. We would contribute this to the way the case has been portrayed in the media; we do not so much question the accuracy of this portrayal, but rather want to express our surprise that a case of deadly use of force has led to such a widespread belief of the innocence of the soldier involved. This may be caused by a changed perception of the world, and the hostility and violence experienced by some right at home in the Netherlands.

Regardless, the view on military violence has changed from the views held in the proverbial 1960s. Such a conclusion would fit in the general picture of social changes that may be taking place in the Netherlands and Western-Europe.

Whom society trusts with the use of force, remains the fulcrum of this discussion in the end. The abstractions used in this essay as well as in legal philosophy or sociology, translate to the level of the individual only to some degree. In the end, we believe that society will have to put its faith in the reasonable officer on the scene, and devise its penal system accordingly. No rules clear enough, or policies strict enough, can change the fact that society consists of individuals such as Eric O., whom we trust to use force when necessary, and only then. What is reasonable is defined at the level of this individual, rather than by his government.

List of References

Articles and books

J.F.R. Boddens Hosang, Rules of Engagement: Het politiek-juridische struikelblok voor de militaire commandant, *Militair Rechtelijk Tijdschrift*, nr. 9, 2003.

F.H. van der Burg, Militair strafrecht zonder nucleaire paraplu, *Nederlands Juristenblad*, 17 september 2004, nr. 33.

G.L. Coolen, *Militair straf- en strafprocesrecht*, 3e druk, Zwolle, W.E.J. Tjeenk Willink, 2000.

G.L. Coolen, '*Geweldsinstructie*' vanuit strafrechtelijk oogpunt bezien, *Militair Rechtelijk Tijdschrift*, nr. 9, 2003.

J.A. van Diepenbrugge, Geweldgebruik in het kader van vredesoperaties: leidt de integratie van politieke, juridische en operationele aspecten in de Rules of Engagement in het kader van vredesoperaties tot vage en multi-interpretabele regels?, *Militair Rechtelijk Tijdschrift*, nr. 9, 2003.

W.J.M. van Genugten, De oorlog in Irak als bijdrage aan het hervormingsdebat binnen de VN, *Militair Rechtelijk Tijdschrift*, afl. 5, 2004.

A.H.M. van Iersel en Th.A van Baarda (red.), *Militaire Ethiek: morele dilemma's van militairen in theorie en praktijk*, Bureau voor Ethiek en Krijgsmacht van Defensie in opdracht van de Staatssecretaris van Defensie, 2002.

N. Jörg, Een opmerking over de reikwijdte van het beroep op ambtelijk bevel en een opmerking over de delictskeuze van de officier van justitie, in militaribus, *Militair Rechtelijk Tijdschrift*, nr. 9, 2003.

G.G.J. Knoops, Rules of Engagement – Internationaalrechtelijke, ethische en operationele implicaties, *Marineblad*, december 2002.

G.G.J. Knoops, De (inter)nationaal strafrechtelijke betekenis en implicaties van *geweldsinstructie*s voor buitenlandse militaire missies, *Delikt en Delinkwent*, nr. 6, 2004.

A.S. Paphiti UK A, Rules of Engagement within multinational land operations, *Militair Rechtelijk Tijdschrift*, nr. 1, 1996.

Rulings

- Rechtbank Arnhem, October 18, 2004, *LJN* AR4029.
- Rechtbank Arnhem, March 1st, 2004, *NJ* 2004/206.
- Hoge Raad, December 23rd, 1980, *MRT* 1981, p. 300.
- Gerechtshof Arnhem, May 4th, 2005, *LJN* AT4988.